Step Aside

SUPER WOMAN

Step Aside

SUPER WOMAN

Christine Brown-Quinn

First Published in Great Britain 2010 by Bookshaker

To Tom, for always believing in me.

Contents

Introduction

WHEN I WAS ASKED to give a talk at the launch event for a business women's network, I decided to focus on one of the biggest issues facing young educated women today: How do I actually make career *and* family work? This gave me a chance to take a brief moment to think about how I was able to combine my own career and family for over twenty years. Before then I hadn't really given it much thought. I just got on with it.

What I realized, as I was putting together my material for the speech, is that the values, strategies and skill sets that enabled me to be successful in my international finance career were *identical* to those needed to balance my active family life (three children - now aged from twenty three to nine – and a husband with an equally demanding career). My other half encouraged me to take these ideas further. "You should write a book," he nudged. At the time I thought he was crazy. Then I realized that by sharing what I'd learned over the years, I might be able to inspire young women to have the confidence to combine their own careers with family. And how could I possibly pass up such an opportunity? This, together with the enthusiastic feedback I've received from hundreds of professional women when discussing this topic, convinced me that writing a book and revealing my own personal thoughts and experiences was a risk worth taking.

Christine Brown-Quinn

CHAPTER ONE

To Understand Today, You
Need To Understand Yesterday

EDUCATED YOUNG WOMEN TODAY are clear about what they want. Combining career goals with family aspirations is a given. They also expect to share the domestic and financial responsibilities of raising a family with their partners. Yes, you can say it loudly and not feel guilty or isolated: *I want both!* Combining career and family is an irreversible, long-term trend resulting from women's tremendous progress in education, professional qualifications and career development over the last four decades. As women progress there is less likelihood that they will give it all up once they have families.

As a young woman you are part of this huge and irreversible trend in the advancement of women. To fully appreciate this, take a look back at your grandmother's, mother's, aunts' or even older sisters' more limited access to higher education or career opportunities. Young women today have independence and opportunities previous generations could only have dreamt of. You are where you are today because of the women who came before you. To give you a true sense of just how dramatic the changes have been over the last forty years, let's take a quick look at some of these mega trends.

MEGA TRENDS CREATED TODAY'S OPPORTUNITIES

What's Happened In Education?

In undergraduate education there are now more females than males in the US, UK, as well as Canada. In the US women receive 57% of bachelors degrees. There's a similar picture in the UK where 55% of undergraduates were female in 2008.

This is a significant change from the 1970s when many universities had just opened their doors to women. Can you believe that? 1970 doesn't seem that long ago.

My sister-in law attended one of the leading universities in the US in the fall of 1968. At that time the ratio of men to women on campus was 10:1. The university was divided into several schools covering a range of concentrations: business, foreign service, nursing, languages as well as a general liberal arts school. In 1968 women were *not* accepted into the business or general liberal arts programs, and this practice was certainly not uncommon at other universities in the US. When the liberal arts program was then opened up to women the following year, my sister-in-law transferred there from the language program so that she could take advantage of a broader range of courses, including music which was one of her special interests.

Once she got into the liberal arts program, there were more doors to be opened. With her keen interest in music, she naturally wanted to join one of the music groups on campus. To her dismay, *none* of the music

2

groups were open to women. She was determined to put things right. Looking at the different resources of the clubs, she decided to focus her efforts on the glee club, which had one of the largest budgets. She then approached a faculty member to discuss the situation. Having shared with him her resolve to get a petition together if necessary (which would include every female student's signature on it), the faculty member conceded to her request. He had a sense that things were changing and felt obliged (and cornered?) to support the effort.

You have to remember that the 60s and early 70s were a time of tremendous social upheaval in America: the Vietnam War, the Women's Liberation Movement and the Sexual Revolution. Anyone witnessing the events and turmoil of the times would have realized that looking backwards would not solve the challenges of the day. It's funny nowadays to think that it took a *women's movement* to gain access to simple privileges like a university education and participation in a music club.

Since the 1980s society has increased its expectations of what girls can achieve. It's almost a self-fulfilling prophecy. Give girls the confidence and opportunity to excel and they do just that. Still more progress, however, needs to be made in changing society's attitudes. Several years ago an English friend shared with me her utter frustration with her other half about educational choices for their son and daughter. She recounted that her husband was okay to invest in their son's private education, but he thought it was a waste of money to pay for a private education for their daughter because she was just that - a *daughter*, a *female.* I found this story shocking and almost unbelievable that it could happen in the 21st century in the developed world. Unfortunately, but not surprisingly, my friend and her husband did eventually split up. If this was what the husband thought of their daughter, what did he think of his own wife? Was she not worth investing in?

What's Happened In The Professional Fields?

Women have entered into traditionally male-dominated professions, such as law and medicine, with a vengeance. In the UK 60% of new solicitors are women. In the US women represent half of all law school students and one third of lawyers. The percentage of female doctors has also been steadily increasing in the UK, US and Canada. Based on current growth trends, women are expected to make up 70% of the doctors in the UK in five years. In the US over 30% of doctors are women, compared to 10% in the 70s. The trend is even more pronounced in US medical schools where 50% of the students are female.

Work practices in these traditionally male-dominated professions are profoundly changing as a result of more and more women entering these fields. Women doctors in the US tend to work 20 to 25% less than their male counterparts. Is this because they are lazy? Of course not. The 60+ hour work week isn't feasible for many female doctors who have children and wish to continue practicing medicine after childbirth. This, combined with the fact that the majority of US female doctors are married to partners who also work 40+ hours a week, makes time at home even more critical.

A similar trend is happening in Canada where female doctors tend not to work the same hours or work for the same number of years as their male counterparts. Perhaps male doctors welcome this change in assumptions about working hours and the number of years in service. It may provide them with the opportunity to become more involved with their own families and create a better balance between work and family.

There are important consequences to these kinds of paradigm shifts. What impact will this have on doctors' work practices, for example, or on the provision of services? As a society we will need to assume that we will need more doctors to take care of the same number of patients if doctors are going to work less. So the question then becomes not *whether* women should participate fully in a professional life, but rather how does society need to adapt now that women *are* participating? I'll come back to these broader implications later.

What's Happened To The Workforce?

The percentage of women in the workforce has changed dramatically over the last forty years. The number of working women worldwide is expected to grow from one billion to 1.2 billion over the next five years. Their annual income is expected to increase over this period from $12 billion to $18 billion. That's a lot of money! Women make up half of the US workforce today compared to one third forty years ago. In Canada there were actually more women than men in paid employment in 2009.

The recession, along with structural changes to the economy, is creating an even greater demand for women to work.

A recent poll by Workingmums.co.uk revealed that more than two thirds of the women surveyed were thinking about increasing their work hours, or shifting from part time to full time, because they are worried about their partners losing their jobs in the recession. The recession has hit the male-dominated industries of construction, manufacturing and finance particularly hard.

The current US "man recession" (four out of five jobs lost in the US over the past two years have been held by men) is in large part due to the shift in the economy from manufacturing to the service sector, which places more value on the feminized skills of multi-tasking and interpersonal communication. Back in the 1980s I came across this gender gap when I worked as a conference producer for a business information firm in London. Over 90% of the employees were women as the job required a high degree of multi-tasking and organizational skills. The managing director and founder of the company at the time commented to me that her female employees demonstrated an ability to multi-task that far exceeded their male counterparts'. The downside for the boss, of course, was that there was always someone on maternity leave.

Women are also increasingly becoming the primary breadwinners. *The Times Magazine* poll conducted in the summer of 2009 showed that 40% of working women in the US are the co- or primary breadwinners. In the UK 20% of wives now earn more than their husbands (a fivefold increase from 1970). The number of stay-at-home dads has increased tenfold in the past decade according to a recent survey conducted by Aviva, the insurance company. The main reason behind this decision to stay at home is simple economics – the mother earned more money.

Another trend accentuated by the recession is the increase in female entrepreneurship. More and more women are starting their own businesses as the traditional job market has become less secure. In the UK more women than men are setting up small businesses; the number of female-led businesses could double from one million to two million over the next ten years, according to the UK's Federation of Small Businesses. A similar pattern has emerged in the US over the last decade. The number of privately-owned companies started by women has increased twice as fast as the number started by men.

Prowess, the UK voice for women's enterprise, has released new research showing that women business owners are driving a new, more robust, feminine enterprise model based on diligent risk taking and collaboration. This model also takes into account the wider social values alongside profits. Women entrepreneurs are also demonstrating that they are innovative, adaptive, empathetic and responsive in this fragile economy. The state of the economy has tipped the balance in women's thinking, spurning them on to take risk and overcome feelings of self doubt.

Technology has, of course, played a major role in making self employment as well as working from home more possible than ever. Running your own business has the added benefit of allowing you to set your own hours to suit your personal needs. Don't be naïve: you'll still need help with caring for your kids even if you run your own business, but you'll have more flexibility in determining *when* you work. Women businesses have now become accepted, with many larger companies outsourcing work to lower costs. This business model focuses on the quality of the work or product delivered, rather than the number of hours worked or where the work was done.

The Impact On Life Expectancy, Marriage, Childbearing And Divorce

The picture wouldn't be complete if I didn't mention what's happened to life expectancy, marriage, childbearing and divorce (sorry, we have to deal with realities, not myths) as women have climbed the professional ladder. If you're in your 20s or 30s, you can expect to live longer than previous generations. You are also more likely to delay or avoid marriage and, as a natural consequence, have children later in life as well. And if you do marry, there's a higher chance that the marriage could end in divorce than would have been the case forty years ago.

It's good news all around for males and females in the UK and US in terms of life expectancy. Life expectancy in the UK has reached its highest level on record for both males and females (seventy seven for males and eighty one for females), although this gap between male and female life expectancies has been narrowing over the past twenty five years (Office for National Statistics). The statistics for the US are similar, with life expectancy of seventy five for males and eighty for females (Centers for Disease Control).

Marriage rates, on the other hand, have been declining for years. The rate has declined in the US by nearly 50% since 1970. Similarly UK weddings are on the decline since their peak in 1972. The decrease in the rate of marriage can be partly explained by the increase in the number of couples living together. At the same time as couples are marrying less, the average age of women who do marry has increased. The average age in the US is twenty nine versus thirty one in the UK. Since women are marrying later, it's no surprise that they are also having children later.

Women in the UK are on average giving birth at twenty nine, compared to twenty six in the late 70s. Childlessness is also on the increase as is motherhood at the age of forty.

While women gained economic power over the last four decades, the divorce rate soared. I'm not a marriage counselor so I certainly won't comment on all the potential reasons for this increase, but I certainly recognize that women's economic independence may have played a factor. The good news is that divorce rates have been stabilizing recently, although you can't ignore the impact that co-habitation has had on this. In 2009 for the first time ever in the UK there were actually more people who were single or living together than married.

It makes sense that women's striking achievements in the academic and professional world must have influenced other areas of society. Is the influence over? Has our society adjusted to the new realities? I think not. Read on.

MORE PROGRESS IS NEEDED

Where Are All The Women Leaders?

While progress in the advancement of women has been enormous, there is still more work to be done. And I'm counting on you to do it. Women are still largely working in the helping professions of health and education and are falling behind in the higher-paying fields of the future: science, math, engineering and technology. Also, there are far too few women among the highest ranks of many professions, despite the increasing size of the female talent pool. It's the upper echelons of organizations and industries where decisions are made. Don't we need women decision makers to ensure that our institutions make objective and well-rounded decisions, reflecting the needs of *all* customers, shareholders and citizens they represent (not just the male ones)?

In business, the proportion of female directors in the UK's FTSE 100 is 12%, which is a meager 5% higher than in 1999. This subject has been given a lot of press attention lately, given the failures of banks and other businesses which have been dominated by (almost exclusively) male boards and key decision makers. Harriet Harman, Deputy Leader of the UK Labour Party at the time of writing, drove this point home when she commented that the collapse of Lehman Brothers may not have happened if it were "Lehman Sisters". Psychological studies suggest that more diversity is better than less when it comes to decision making, innovation and problem solving. In today's globally competitive economy, capitalizing on only half the talent pool surely doesn't make business sense.

Although females represent over 50% of the US population, women are under-represented in the halls of Congress and the boardrooms of corporate America. The US Bureau of Statistics reported in 1979 that on average women made 62 cents for every dollar men made. Still today the average American woman only earns 80% of what an average American man makes.

Old Habits Die Hard

Given that career and family is not a temporary phenomenon, but rather an expanding one, all aspects of our society need to acknowledge this new reality. The old assumption that a mother is home and a father is the breadwinner is out of touch with today's diverse family structures and roles. The practices and policies of our businesses, schools, government and religious institutions need to adjust to the new structure. And it's not only at an institutional level where changes are needed. Even within personal settings such as families, neighborhoods and social circles, older generations (and some younger) may hold onto attitudes about family structures that are stuck in days gone by. Old habits die hard.

Schools and churches have been slow to respond to the reality that women are increasingly employed outside of the home. Many schools still adhere to timetables that completely disregard the demands of working parents. Churches have also been slow to take advantage of the female talent available for leadership roles rather than simply supporting roles. Timings of school and church meetings often clash with working hours, increasingly limiting both men and women's involvement in these institutions.

Although policies (maternity leave, paternity leave and flexible working) have been changing in the US and the UK to recognize that *people* (not just women) have work *as well as* family commitments, there is still a stigma attached to men taking advantage of these policies. It is also not widely accepted that men have good reason to work part-time. Given that many women opt for part-time work following childbearing, they have been impacted the most by the assumption that part-time work means part-time commitment.

Many institutions talk the talk, but don't walk the walk. They give lip service to the idea that women are adept leaders and managers, while at the same time following old habits which prevent women from excelling. Here's a wonderful illustration of this point. You would have thought that a private girls' school that promoted leadership qualities in their exclusively female student body would be the first to recognize such changes. But no…

At 16 my daughter was interviewing for a place at such a school. She was horrified to hear the female principal comment during her interview that she needed to make the most out of the education that her *father* was paying for. How ironic! A school dedicated to developing future female leaders assumes that only dads earn money to pay the bills. The principal's views were still based on the assumption that there was only one type of family structure. In the end, my daughter decided against this school because of, among other things, its backward-looking culture.

Sometimes it's hard to believe that these old views of what the family looks like still persist. I was astonished by the outdated ways of thinking that my friend the IT programmer faced when he was hired by a local school to install a new management information system. The new system had been built by two of the school's former male students and was gaining a reputation as being cutting edge within the local educational circles. After having downloaded the school's data into the new software, my friend ran a few tests. He just couldn't understand how a school with over 1,000 pupils only had information being distributed to females when it pertained to the school's activities. This was what the database was telling him.

He then ran another test, but this time only selecting information that was being distributed in connection with tuition bills. These results were equally puzzling. It appeared that the tuition bills were only going to males.

My friend is married to a marketing guru and entrepreneur and the couple has two teenage children. With this personal background, he was astounded that these two twenty year olds viewed society along these strict dividing lines.

Personally I have encountered similar characterize-ations over the years. When my older son was about ten, he was trying to pay me a compliment when he observed, "I know how things work in our family. You organize the vacations and Dad pays for them." I felt like a stake had been driven through my heart. Given the long hours and travel I endured to succeed professionally and provide financial stability to our family, how could he say such a thing? The blood, sweat and tears for sticking with a fiercely competitive and aggressive environment, for what? Deep breath. "Okay he's only ten, let's think about this logically," I said to myself. I then asked him what he thought I did when I went to work all day. Complete silence. He was obviously getting external messages (The media? Friends at school?) that this was the way families operated, even though his own family clearly did not work that way.

Old pockets of thinking are easier to accept, or at least understand, when they come from the older generations. In the early 90s an elderly neighbor invited me to join a knitting club on Wednesday afternoons, which was a very kind gesture given that we had just moved in. "Thank you for the kind invitation, but I work full time in London," I replied. Her reaction took me completely off guard. "What a shame!" she exclaimed. Not, "That's fantastic that you can do that and have a family. That would not have been possible in my day." The conversation left me feeling disappointed and deflated.

Stepping back and looking at the shifts in attitude *over a longer horizon,* however, gives me courage. There have certainly been significant changes in societal attitudes from generation to generation. My mom always said I could be vice president of a company. I, on the other hand, thought why should I settle on vice president, what's wrong with president? Her mother (my grandmother), by contrast, assumed without any doubt that my mother would stay home when starting a family.

I'm at the tail end of the baby boomers and one could argue that it's my generation that has had the first *real* choice in combining career and family, both in terms of opportunities as well as attitudes. It was the age group between me and my mother who were lighting the fire under the women's liberation movement. While I've tended to have the perception that the women's lib movement was radical and included men haters (and I certainly am not one of them), I do accept that it's the hard work of those women which catapulted my generation into a position of enjoying the benefits of a more equal workplace.

Creating New Habits

Recent research shows that it's the younger generation that is more likely to share responsibilities for economic security as well as childrearing than the older generations. (No way could I imagine my dad changing diapers, but yes my husband mastered the skill.) The recession is also making inroads into how society *thinks* about women and working. Men are becoming more involved in the daily responsibilities of childrearing partly as a result of loss or reduction of employment, but men's attitudes about their own roles are changing. The UK Equality and Human Rights Commission's research shows that most fathers with full-time jobs would rather spend more time bringing up their children. Dads today equate being a good father with "being there" and spending time with their kids, rather than just being the breadwinner according to a new study released by Boston College's Center for Work & Family.

Although I get frustrated when people try to box me into a certain stereotype, I have a lot of sympathy for those men who have taken the decision, along with their other halves, that they will become the *primary* caregivers. This lifestyle choice is even less accepted than women taking on the leading breadwinner role. I can only imagine how isolated these men may feel at times. This type of family structure has arisen partly as a result of the recession, but also as a result of the promotion of women into senior positions within business and government. The Governor of Michigan, Jennifer Granholm, and her husband demonstrate how this type of family structure can work. Like any other successful team or partnership they've worked out who's doing what, showing ultimate respect for each other's "lanes". More about teams later. The Governor's husband, who like herself is a Harvard Law School graduate, has taken on the leading role in raising their three children so that his wife can pursue her political ambitions.

As more leaders and managers appreciate the new realities of family life, it becomes easier to manage the logistics of career and family. David Gregory, host of the American program, *Meet the Press*, commented during an interview with Maria Shriver (former First Lady of the State of California and member of the Kennedy family) that he has found it easier to juggle his career and family commitments because he has a female boss who understands how his family structure works. He has two daughters and is married to a top-notch trial lawyer, so he needs to coordinate his travel schedule, for example, with his wife's before he can commit. His boss fully understands this need.

With this nostalgic perspective it becomes clearer that your desire to pursue career goals *as well as* family aspirations is part of an evolutionary process. As a young woman there has never been a better time to achieve career-family success. Many trends are working in your favor. Now let's move on to the secret formula. How do I make it all work?

To Understand Today, You Need To Understand Yesterday

CHAPTER TWO

Getting The Balance Right for You

ONE SIZE DOESN'T FIT ALL

WHAT DOES BALANCE MEAN? Does it mean that everything is always operating at equilibrium and the scales are perfectly in line at every moment? Most certainly not. Think of balance by looking at your life from the outside in. Is your work and home life integrated, blending and shifting in a way that you're happy with? While I can offer suggestions, I cannot tell you what precise combination of career and family works best for you. Each of us has our own needs and desires. I happened to have had my first set of children early in my marriage and therefore was just starting out in my career. I had endless amounts of energy at twenty six and twenty nine, when I had my first two children. For me there was no doubt I would continue to pursue my career with vigor. I was realistic, though no less determined, that not everything always goes to plan. I knew I had to remain flexible and deal with whatever surprises life had in store for me.

This lifestyle of continuing a demanding career after short maternity breaks worked for me and my family, but this mix is not suited to everyone. You need to find out what works for *you* and *your* family, remembering that the path of least resistance – you completely giving up your own career ambitions – is not necessarily the best option for you or your family in the long run. Unfortunately, life is much more complicated than that.

There are advantages and disadvantages of having children when you're younger, so there's no *right* answer to when it's best to start a family. Of course this will also depend on how early you find the right partner, if you haven't already, or whether you decide to go it alone. Earlier means it's easier to conceive, harder to afford convenient childcare, but perhaps easier to juggle it all as you have a lot more energy. Had I not had other children before having my third child at forty, I think it might have been more difficult to imagine keeping up the pace of both my family and professional life. It would have been more of a shock to the system. On the other hand, having a child at forty took out some of the stress of having to prove myself at work (I had already done that so having a child wasn't an indication that I wasn't committed) and I also had more resources to lessen the worries of childcare and the burden of household chores.

What's The Right Balance For You?

What's the right balance for you? One size does not fit all. At a high level, you could say that balance is when you feel like you are contributing professionally (making a difference to an organization or industry and not just collecting a pay check) as well as participating meaningfully in raising a family. It depends on how you *feel*, not the absolute levels of involvement in either career or family. You'll know it's working when positive energy generated from your work carries over into the home and vice versa.

The two dimensions of your life can improve the overall quality of your one life. That's right. Career and family can be *complementary* rather than in conflict. Because you are experiencing both environments, you tend to appreciate more the intellectual challenge and camaraderie that the work environment provides. Conversely, you may appreciate more the spiritual and emotional fulfillment and bigger-picture perspective that your family life gives you. Having different dimensions in your life can help you step back and view problems in a new light and give you a completely fresh outlook. When I worked on a trading floor I used to arrive for work religiously at 7am, usually in a good mood and eager to get down to business. I often commented to colleagues that it was great to be back to work, especially after a vacation or long weekend. This puzzled some of my colleagues until of course they started having families themselves. Then they got it. Taking care of a family is hard work, physically and mentally.

Keep Steady in Your Beliefs

In the end, what you decide might seem crazy to others. Ignore them. Do what's right for *you*. As time goes on, you might make different choices. There is nothing wrong with that. In fact, it may give you the courage to make decisions as you'll know you can always make different decisions later. Remember you always have options and the right answer for one stage in your life may not necessarily be the right answer for another stage.

Sometimes the reaction of others to your choices can be (unintentionally) painful. Keep steady in *your* beliefs.

A marketing colleague shared with me her own experience of this phenomenon when I explained to her my theory that there is no way one size can fit all. She remembers very vividly the Sunday lunch when her guest openly commented about the choices she had made about how to balance career and family. "I don't know how you can leave your adorable son with someone else all day," the guest remarked. Argh! A stab in the heart! She described her reaction as one of disbelief, followed by an aching pain. She couldn't agree more that her son was an adorable toddler, but was that the only rationale for being with him all day? The decision to leave your child in someone else's care is much more complex.

My colleague's guest was also a mother and she happened to have made different choices about how to get the balance right between work and family. No problem there. As a nurse she was able to do shift work in the evening which meant that her kids' schedule could be completely accommodated. This obviously isn't possible for many other professions. The career and family combination comes in many different varieties. Different strokes for different folks. Don't judge others or feel judged by others (I know it's hard). You've got to find the balance that works for you, not for your friend, not your colleague, not even for your mother. You've got to be true to yourself.

Greater Choices On The Shape Of Career & Family

When I talk about career and family I get *really* excited about the future for younger women. There are more choices than ever before on how to shape what the combination of career and family will look like – many more than when I started out on this path over twenty years ago. I am very jealous. Entrepreneurship and the ability to work from home, largely enabled by technology, have created many more possibilities. Because of the influx of women into traditionally male-dominated professions, it is now possible to work less than a sixty hour week in these fields as well as to progress to senior management levels.

It would have been unheard of twenty years ago for a woman to become a partner in a large accounting firm and work a reduced schedule in order to accommodate child rearing. Offering flexible or non-traditional work schedules enable women (and men) to continue to contribute to their profession despite demanding personal commitments such as young children or caring for an elderly parent.

The belief in the benefits of diversity has encouraged many professional service firms to develop and support programs aimed at fostering and retaining female talent. Some firms have even established programs specifically aimed at supporting women to reach the upper echelons of their organizations - partner and board level ranks, not just managers. This is the next push needed in the advancement of women: assisting them to become decision makers, not just well-respected professionals.

NO NEED FOR A GUILT TRIP

One of the biggest challenges to deal with when you resume work after childbirth is often the guilt trip. There is *no* need for this. Put your logic hat on and consider the facts. Your child will need to learn sooner or later that he or she is part of a larger world. The sooner they learn about working as part of a team the better. Children need to learn to become independent. They need to learn social and organizational skills in order to survive in the real world. You won't be around forever to sort things out for them.

The interesting thing about being a parent is that your child has an incredibly keen sense of how *you* are feeling. If you are worried, they are likely to be worried. Conversely, if you are happy, your child has a greater chance of being happy. When your child reaches school age, his or her teacher will sometimes ask you what's going on at home because they seem unsettled at school. This special bond between parent and child is one of the overriding reasons why you should look after yourself. If you are not happy and healthy, you won't be doing yourself or your family any good at all.

Although everyone has good days and bad days, I have to say that most of the time I am ready to inspire and motivate my kids at the end of my work day because I've been motivated and inspired. Being fulfilled in my own work gives me the energy to give back to others. It refills my gas tank. Don't get me wrong, I have bad days too. My mother used to refer to these as "stones". But that's just one day. You'll have many more "diamond" days if you're striking the right balance. My bad days are the ones when my nine year old observes, "Mom, you're in a really bad mood today." This comment gives me the jolt I need and makes me realize that it's unfair to take it out on a young child. Yes, he does take it out on me sometimes, but as the adult I'm supposed to behave better.

Quality Time Is NOT A Myth

When your child spends time away from you, you become more conscious and deliberate about *how* you spend your time when you're with your child. You take it less for granted. You make it count more. Quality time is not a myth. Also *make* time. Delegate or forget about the more trivial household tasks so you have time for the important things in life. You need to be vigilant about spending time together – schedule it in and stick to it – and discuss with your children how they would like to spend the time.

Choices, choices, choices. In a professional environment, let's be honest, you could work twenty four hours a day, seven days a week and everything that needed to be done still wouldn't be done. Is it worth doing this to the detriment of your health, your marriage and your children? Who would want to be around you anyway in that kind of state? You're likely to be tired and irritable. And who's going to be around for you in your hour of need, when you're old or sick? When I worked in finance, there were often events in the evening on top of the normal ten hour day. After-work drinks for people leaving the firm, or otherwise, were commonplace. I was extremely selective about which events I attended, even though I'm sure all of them would have benefited my professional life in one way or another. It just wasn't worth the sacrifice for my family. For me it was a compromise well worth taking. There are always choices to be made. It's part of being human. There just isn't enough time on the earth to pursue all the things you want to pursue. Whichever lifestyle you pursue, there always will be a shortage of time. There is no need to feel guilty about that. It's not your fault.

Nothing Worthwhile Comes Easy

Can you think of anything that's easy in your life that you would consider incredibly satisfying? Isn't it true that the harder you have to work at something, the more gratifying the end result is? The truth is nothing worthwhile comes easy. This applies equally to balancing career and family. While it is incredibly gratifying, it is not easy. To be successful at the balancing act you have to have a high degree of creativity. You create ways to move around what may be perceived as roadblocks. To do this, a *can do* attitude is a prerequisite. If you don't think you can do it, you won't.

I can guarantee that you will face obstacles and reasons to throw it all in – considerable time pressures, sleepless nights with young children, deadlines at work coinciding with family commitments… the list is probably endless. One of the biggest and most important challenges you will face will be finding suitable childcare. You might find the perfect option, but the hours don't match your work hours. You'll worry about trusting a third party to take care of your child. These challenges are not insurmountable. You can overcome them if you take the right approach.

SOLVING FOR THE "CHILDCARE EQUATION"

By doing the prep work, you can take a lot of the worry out of the childcare conundrum. Approach this challenge like any other significant challenge you have tackled. Be determined that you will find the right provider and do your homework. Get feedback on the potential candidate or nursery school from references. Also chat informally with other parents, visiting the childcare facility or provider's home unannounced to see how happy and settled the children are. Always get at least two references and speak to them *personally*. For such an important decision, you don't want to rely on someone else to do the checking. Other people's checks should be in addition to, not instead of, your own due diligence.

When you're speaking to a referee, ask what are the three characteristics you like the most about the person, and what are the three characteristics you like the least and why. What areas could be improved? How reliable has the provider been? Is she a good communicator? Does she raise issues as soon as they come up or wait until they get to breaking point? Try to ask open-ended questions. You'd be surprised what people are willing to tell you. Follow your instinct and intuition.

Leverage The Knowledge & Views Of Your "Home Team"

Similar to your work environment, leverage the knowledge and views of those around you: your other half, older siblings, other babysitters who may be providing some support. They represent your core home team and will offer different perspectives. Involve them in the decision making process. Two or more heads are definitely better than one. You also need to build consensus so that when the new arrangement is in place, everyone is trying to make it work.

Having experienced a number of nanny interviews, my daughter at the age of seven was well prepared to take part in the interviewing process. During one such interview she sat on the high-back Queen Ann chair in the living room with her legs crossed and proceeded with her line of questioning: "You know, my mom will ask you to run errands as well – take the shirts to the drycleaners, buy groceries and take packages to the post office." The questioning continued for about five minutes. My daughter forgot to add, of course, that the nanny would have to deal with my daughter's stubbornness now and again, but hey, I'd say that was a pretty thorough interview for a seven year old. Sometimes you think that kids are just playing in the background, but they're not. They're taking in every word, watching every move. They know exactly what's going on. Capitalize on this. Take advantage of having them be part of the process and the solution going forward.

Before you interview a candidate, it's very useful to write down a checklist of the kind of things you are expecting from the person: what are the duties? Also outline your philosophy: what's most important to you? If you have someone in your home, is keeping the house tidy more important than homework? If your child is being cared for outside of your home, what are the kids eating? What's their method or approach when children misbehave? This is a really important question. If you agree with the approach, you want to adopt a similar approach at home to provide consistency. Children learn more quickly what's right and what's wrong when they are subjected to a consistent set of rules.

Be Clear About Your Requirements

Whatever your arrangement, once you hire someone it's always a good idea to put an agreement in place. It doesn't necessarily have to be formal, although nowadays formal agreements are more common. When I started down this track, there was no such thing as an agreement. I used to put together a *memorandum of understanding*, which was considered to be forward thinking at the time. Even if the childcare provider has her own agreement or requirements, it's still helpful for you to share your written comments. It will help you crystallize your own thoughts and then communicate your priorities. You should have a good understanding about how public holidays are handled. Also, what happens if the childcare provider is ill? What happens if enough staff aren't available on a given day at the nursery school? What are the back-up plans?

Here's a sample of the outline I used when interviewing for a nanny for our younger son. It may give you some ideas about how to approach your own situation. The concepts work equally well whether you're leaving your child at a nursery or the childcare provider's home (which I also did for many years).

- **Requirements:** live-in, non-smoker, driver, experienced with references
- **Start date:** as soon as possible
- **Accommodation:** own room with en-suite bath
- **Key aspects of the role:**
  - *Take/collect our son to/from school*
  - *Supervise homework*
  - *Take our son to/from tennis lessons*
  - *Prepare evening meal for our son (can do large meal - Mom and Dad will eat leftovers!)*
  - *Do light housework – keep house tidy, take care of family laundry (cleaner comes once a week)*
  - *Run errands – buy groceries, drop off items to shoe repair/dry cleaner, buy stamps at post office etc.*
- **Holidays:** all national holidays, plus five weeks per year (at full pay) – taken at the same time as the family holiday(s)
- **Hours:** Monday – Friday
- **Pay:** commensurate with experience/ qualifications
- **Babysitting:** occasionally need after 7.30pm or weekends
- **Commitment:** minimum 1 year and 6 weeks notice

- **General:** as both my husband and I work full time, we kindly request at least six weeks notice before nanny terminates employment (of course if we were able to find a replacement earlier, the nanny would be welcome to leave earlier)

Regardless of the care you and your team finally decide on, put in place plan b, c, d and e. No joke. There will be times when the provider will call in sick, the daycare centre will be closed or your child will be unwell. Get agreement in the front end from friends, relatives or part-time babysitters about when you can call upon them for these emergencies.

Think About Your Childcare Costs Over A Longer Horizon

The other challenge with childcare is obviously the cost. I agree it's not cheap. Don't think that just because I was able to afford a nanny later in life that I don't understand how expensive childcare can be. It's a considerable expense, especially when you're younger. To get your head around this one, you need to consider a couple of key points. Firstly, consider that your career/job should only be funding 50% of the cost; the father's career/job pays for the other 50%. This is particularly important if you've just finished school and you're starting out. Otherwise, you could become quickly discouraged. Secondly, remember that when you are in the earlier years of your career, the cost as a percentage of your income is high, but this then decreases as you progress in your career. Your earnings are likely to increase at a much faster rate than the cost of the childcare. To reduce the costs, you can also think about sharing childcare arrangements with friends and neighbors or recruiting grandparents.

Think of your career as providing a *stream* of future income, not just a fixed amount at this point in time (apologies for the financial jargon, I can't help it). Also remember that once your child goes to school, the cost of childcare decreases, although at that point you may want to consider private schools. My advice is to keep investing in that career so that you have *choices* in the future. Private school may not be necessary or the right option for your child, but your career progression puts you in a position to at least have that option.

Bring All Your Skills & Positive Outlook To Bear To Find Good Childcare

The essential ingredient to finding childcare that matches your family's needs is to be positive and tenacious. At the age of thirty I went back to school full-time in the US for an MBA. At that time we had two kids, ages one and four. The nannies in the US were more expensive than and not as common as in the UK where we had previously lived, so the affordable option was to find a childcare provider who worked in her own home. All of the providers adhered to pretty strict working hours. The starting times did vary a bit, but the consensus for finishing time was absolutely no later than 6pm. The problem was that some of my classes were in the evening and there was no way my other half could manage a 6pm pick up. I continued the childcare search with the belief that it would work out.

Lo and behold, I then met Aggie, the angel! I explained my predicament and told her that two days a week I needed the kids to stay with her until my husband got home from work, which would be about 7.30pm. She had been running a childcare business in her basement for years and had a very set routine. Despite this, she responded, "I really respect you for going back to school. I'll make an exception to my normal hours for you." More great stories on Aggie later. Our relationship exhibited a number of qualities that really made the career-family balancing act manageable and fun. I could probably write a whole book on just childcare so I'd better stop here. The key message is you can find good childcare, but you'll need to bring all your skills and positive mental outlook to bear.

WHERE ARE THE ROLE MODELS?

Unlike successful men, many successful professional women at the top of their field do not have families. They had to make sacrifices in order to pursue their career ambition. Perhaps even fewer role models in their day discouraged them from following the path of career and family. How unfair is that? Is this the kind of tradeoff that has to be made? It most certainly was the case forty, thirty, or even twenty years ago, but it isn't the case today. More role models are surfacing across a wider range of sectors and organizational levels as more and more women continue to push the boundaries for advancement while also fulfilling their family aspirations.

Having decided which lifestyle you want to follow, you can expect family and friends to give you their two cents worth on what you should or should not be doing. This may be true even if they themselves have no direct expertise. Keep this in mind when you consider whether their opinion is valid. With so few role models comes self doubt. *Can* I do it? *How* do I do it? Yes, you *can* do it. Not only can you do it, but when you do it, everyone around you can benefit from your chosen lifestyle. Intrigued? I hope so. More on this in the next chapter.

WORK-LIFE BALANCE MEANS MUCH MORE THAN FLEXIBLE WORKING

Work-life balance is much more than maternity, paternity leave or flexible working. This view is too one dimensional and focuses on the *me* - what *I* get, without any mention of what I give. There are two sides of the coin – rights *and* responsibilities. When I was doing research for this book, I googled "work-life balance" and to my horror, there was an overwhelming amount of material relating to employee rights and very little about employee responsibilities. The literature was so lopsided that it scared me away from using the term "work-life balance" at all. Most people assume there is too much work and too little balance. Once again, life is more complex than this. You need to consider this issue from many viewpoints in order to truly achieve long-term stability.

Your Responsibility Starts Before Maternity Leave

What are the employee's responsibilities when it comes to work-life balance? In the first instance, taking responsibility means considering how your job will be covered before you start maternity leave. The employee taking the leave should feel like she owns the shortage the organization will suffer while she is away. Who will cover this gap? The person taking the leave should play a major part in organizing and training the maternity cover as she is best placed to know what's required. If you don't believe this is the case, then why should the employer feel a responsibility for you? It works both ways. You will appreciate this even more after you've worn the shoes of the employer/manager as well as the employee.

When to Start Your Maternity Leave

That first pregnancy was tough. I had awful morning sickness. No, correction: I had morning, afternoon and night sickness! I always kept a plastic bag in my purse for emergencies. My husband, like any caring partner, would say, "I don't know how you're going to continue to be able to work through your pregnancy. You seem not to feel well most of the time." I planned on working up until labor pains. My rationale for this seemingly irrational decision was to keep my mind off the nausea and discomfort from carrying all that extra weight. But ol' stubborn me, I would snap back at him, "I am continuing – end of discussion." Mornings were the worst, especially as soon as I woke up. But the thought of crawling back into bed and feeling sorry for myself, and thinking about how awful I felt wasn't very appealing either. Once I made it through the first twenty minutes of the morning, I had confidence I could make it through the rest of the day with the help of salted crackers and a few sips of ginger ale.

The morning sickness did improve after the first trimester and that gave me an added boost of self-assurance to continue working right up until the big day. "Why go earlier?" I thought, "What was I going to do at home?" Just relaxing wasn't one of my strong points. This approach suited me to a tee, but thinking back I probably made a number of colleagues feel uneasy. "When is this lady going to get out of here?" they probably wondered. I'm not suggesting at all that you take a similar approach to when your maternity leave should start. You will need to consider the physical demands of your job as well as your own health. Whatever you do, however, don't leave your organization high and dry! Plan, plan, plan.

Stay In Touch With Your Colleagues – Out Of Sight Is Out Of Mind

Once the leave has started, should you forget about what happens in the workplace? It's someone else's problem now, right? Not quite. I personally believe that when an employee takes maternity leave, except in extreme circumstances such as a serious illness, the employee needs to take responsibility for staying relevant to the organization. Out of sight can be out of mind. Keep in touch with your colleagues and your profession during your leave. If you are in a client service business, it's critical to keep in touch with your colleague who is covering your clients while you're away to ensure a smooth transition. Wouldn't you want him or her to offer the same courtesy if you were the one providing the cover? The person providing the cover will need to quickly get up to speed with new details and aspects of the job. Forget about what the law says. Show respect for your colleagues. Do what's right for your clients and for the business.

As with everything there is a balance. If you were fielding calls and emails all day during your leave, you wouldn't be taking the time you need to recover and look after your new baby. On the other hand, if you don't take *any* calls and stay completely out of touch you are making it very difficult, not only for your colleagues, but also for yourself. If you want to reintegrate back into your prior role, no one is better placed to make that happen than you. Reading professional journals (even the newspaper) is also a good way of keeping up with what's going on - and possibly a welcome break from motherly duties. Stay in touch with not only your boss, but also your colleagues on a more informal basis. Schedule a few lunches or after-work drinks so that you can keep in touch. It will be well worth the investment and will also get you used to the idea of leaving your kids in someone else's care before you go back to work. Consider it to be a practice run.

Communicate Your Plans To Return To Work

Above all, be clear and communicate as soon as possible about what your commitment will be on return from leave so that the impact can be properly dealt with. Your commitment should be backed up with your own planning and preparation for childcare, arrangements with significant other etc. An accountant friend, who works at a prestigious golf club, shared with me her frustration about young women who think they are going to return to work without any planning. She recently interviewed a candidate for an accountancy role who was re-entering the workforce after a maternity break. The candidate wanted to find a position which was more closely linked to her degree than her previous position, and find a location which was closer to home. When my friend asked her when she could start, the candidate replied that she hadn't yet considered what childcare arrangements might be suitable. "What? You're kidding," thought my friend, "I've just spent a whole hour with you and you don't even know when you can start? You haven't even *considered* your childcare options?" I don't think I need to tell you the outcome of that interview.

My other half thought I was nuts when I started looking for childcare five months before our first child was born. At twenty six I was very energetic and ambitious (yes, it's ok to be ambitious and to be a woman) and I knew that I wanted to go back to work quickly after childbirth. It seemed to me that the best thing I could do to show my employer that I was serious about coming back to work was to organize our childcare arrangements. The first question you tend to get asked once you become pregnant is, "What will you do with the baby?" I was fully prepared for this question: I could demonstrate that I had carefully thought through the logistics of our new family dynamics and made plans accordingly. It was a good feeling, and I *was* consequently taken seriously.

Think Like A Business Owner When Returning To Your Working Life

I have seen maternity leave work – i.e. the mother goes on leave and comes back and is able to integrate into her prior role or organization – and I have seen it fail. It fails when the employee thinks, "It's not my problem. The law says I get my job back, or an equivalent, when I come back to work. End of story." Maternity leave and returning to work after childbirth work best when employees *think like business owners*. What would you think and how would you behave if it was your own business?

If you are looking to reduce your hours when you come back to work, think about your needs, but also think about what works best for the business. If you want to change your hours, think about how the business will operate in your absence and what the clients require. If the business operates from 7am until 6pm, don't kid yourself that nine to five is a full day and it will have no impact on the business or the clients. Take ownership for and be creative about the new working arrangement you are hoping to achieve. Be realistic about the demands your reduced or changed hours will have on colleagues and think about how this can be addressed. By following these simple steps you will be able to make a proposal on how to re-enter the organization that is achievable and realistic.

A number of professional women have shared with me their disappointment on returning to work only to find that they have been assigned a bogus, unchallenging role. They have been intentionally sidelined, leading them to start to wonder, "Maybe I should have another child before I leave this place?" This is a vicious circle because employers then lose confidence that after childbirth women will stay committed to employment in the long run. If this happens to you, use your professional network to identify how you can enhance your role. Then approach your boss about your ideas. Articulate your goals and ambition. Take control of your destiny.

Get Buy-In From Your Colleagues On Your New Schedule

When a colleague suggested working shorter hours post her maternity leave, I proposed that she speak with the other members of our group and work out how, as a team, they could make this happen. Getting buy-in in the beginning for a new way of doing things is always easier than trying to build consensus later. This way everyone's pulling in the same direction from day one.

The new work arrangement was successful because the team supported it, and technology made it possible: remote access to the company server, blackberries, and cell phones. Like anything, there were teething problems in the beginning, but we all worked through those, being honest and direct with one another. Occasionally my colleague wanted to leave earlier than her agreed (revised) timetable. She would approach me to share every detail about why she needed to leave early. "Johnny has to get his vaccinations shots. Grandma is going to meet me at the train station with Johnny to make the end-of-day appointment, but I'll still need to leave earlier because..," she would explain.

After several of these episodes, I responded in exasperation, "As your manager I just need to know how you're getting on with your projects and whether there is anything you need from me or the team. Are there any specific issues I should be aware of? I'm not a mean person, really I'm not, but I can't possibly keep track of your family's comings and goings. I'm sure *you're* completely on top of that. I've got enough to remember with my own family!" We both had a chuckle after that outburst and she did adjust her communication style subsequently. The focus of our dialogue needed to be on the professional responsibilities, which she did in fact have covered, but just hadn't thought about making those the heart of the conversation with her manager.

Be Realistic About The Impact Of Reduced Hours On Your Career Opportunities

If you make the decision to reduce your hours, you also need to be realistic about the learning opportunities you will miss. That's not to say that you shouldn't reduce your hours, as that may be necessary for you to strike the balance *you* need. My point is you have to deal with the *commercial* realities of that decision. Also be honest with yourself about how you use the extra time. Are you spending quality time with your child, or are you now taking on the lion's share of household chores in exchange for a shortened professional week? Make sure the tradeoff makes sense personally, professionally and financially.

As a manager I have found it challenging to keep bright women on an upward career path when they frequently worked from home or reduced hours as they wouldn't be around when I needed to pull somebody in on an interesting problem that had to be solved exactly at that moment. In some environments certain issues need to be addressed *now*, never later, never tomorrow.

There's nothing "wrong" with the choice of reduced hours or working from home, as long as you are realistic about the possible consequences. Perhaps your line of work doesn't require as much of a physical presence as a trading floor operation. So again, just think about the potential impact. In life there are a lot of tradeoffs and you will need to decide what makes sense for you. In this particular case my colleague understood that she would miss out on learning opportunities (we chatted about it). She knew that I wasn't intentionally leaving her out of things or excluding her. She was grateful that she could continue to work in a challenging role post maternity leave, even if it meant that she would miss out on certain opportunities.

Whatever Your Choices, Remember Your Priorities

Whatever choices you make, remember your priorities:

1. Your health (you need to look after yourself for your family)
2. Your family
3. Your job/career

Prevention is the Best Medicine

Make sure you're recharging your battery and going for medical check-ups as often as recommended for your age group. This busy lifestyle requires stress relief. Exercise is a wonderful outlet, but maybe that's not the right outlet for you. Find the activity that suits you. It will go a long way in preserving your physical and *mental* health. Your stress relief could be as simple as walking.

With the check-ups you may think, "Oh, they do take a lot of time, I feel fine."Prevention takes up a lot less time than suffering through an illness.

I remember encouraging a male colleague (who had three young kids and a wife who had a number of health issues) to take advantage of the free check-ups the company health plan offered. He felt that his work and personal life were too hectic to take time for things such as check-ups. I kept "nudging" him, and reminding him that he's not only doing it for himself, but also for his family. "You work long hours. That's why the company provides these types of services. You should take advantage of them," I persisted. He conceded in the end and was able to make a few minor, but effective changes to his lifestyle off the back of the doctor's advice, which improved his health considerably. Remember that these check-ups become even more important the older you get. Prevention is the best medicine. Just do it.

Review Your Priorities In The Larger Context

The numbering of the priorities above is intentional. Your health is the most important one. And that does come before your family. Without a healthy you, your family suffers. And family does come before your job/career. Does this mean in every conflict between family and career, family wins out. It absolutely does not mean that. These priorities have to be considered in the bigger picture. At any one particular moment, career might have to take priority over family or vice versa.

It's Sunday evening and you've got an enormously important presentation tomorrow morning. Should you review your notes, or spend that extra hour reading with your child. Career will probably win out, unless you aren't really bothered about keeping your job or being promoted. On the other hand, if your career is constantly interrupting or taking away precious family time, you need to consider whether this is going to be a temporary situation or last indefinitely. If it's going to be indefinite, you need to consider other career/job options.

You may be working on a special three-week project. During those three weeks, your scheduled time at the health club, for instance, may be impacted. This may be okay in the short term, but if you found that you rarely were able to exercise, you need to consider other career/job options. Finding time to exercise is often cited as one of the key reasons for people wanting to work from home. They exchange their commuting time for exercise. Even though our career/job is important there will be other times when you just can't compromise on the demands of the family, even if it's just for the short run. Teacher consultation meetings shouldn't be missed, especially if your child is having problems at school. Every once in a while, take a minute to look at your life in larger view. Ask yourself, "Are my priorities on the whole in order?" If not, it's time to make some changes.

CAREER-FAMILY BALANCE IS DYNAMIC: A CONTINUUM NOT A FIXED POINT IN TIME

Ah, you've got the balance right. Deep sigh of relief. You relish the moment and think this is *wonderful*. I have found peace among the chaos. Yes, it is wonderful, but your circumstances won't stay the same forever. Think of balance as more of a continuum, rather than being a fixed point in time. Why does it keep moving? There is probably an indefinite number of possibilities; that's the way life is. Let me try to outline a few. You may be offered new career opportunities or your other half may take on new responsibilities at his work. More kids may come on the scene. And kids are dynamic in and of themselves. They're always growing and their needs and interests are constantly changing and developing. Changes in employment opportunities and the size of your family result in other changes. Maybe you need to move house, city, or country even. Maybe you decide to put your child in private education now that your salary has increased on the back of your promotion. As one part of your life changes, the other parts move as well in order to bring the whole back to equilibrium.

Don't Confuse Flexibility With Giving Up Your Own Ambition

In a dynamic environment, flexibility is vital. If you're too rigid, what happens when the parts start moving around you, but you don't adjust? You snap. Not only do your circumstances change, but the *you* inside of you changes. Your needs and wants change over time. What's important to you at twenty five isn't what's important to you at forty five. The same applies for your family members. Although you need to remain flexible, don't be too flexible. Don't give up things you *really* want: your ambition and who you are. Doing this might seem to solve tensions in the short term, when you feel like you're being pulled in a million different directions. You think, "If I don't go for what I really want to pursue, it will make the situation easier for others." It's an illusion. It's merely a short-term fix. It's often not sustainable. The danger with that tactic is that problems may surface later in your relationships. It's better to bear the pain momentarily, work things out, than risk damaging the relationship in the long run.

Career Choices Are Challenging For Dual-Career Families

When I finished my MBA seventeen years ago, I asked my other half, "Should I look for a job in Washington DC, NY or London?" "Go for it!" he cheered. He encouraged me to send my resume out *everywhere*. After many months of methodical and assertive networking, I was offered an opportunity to move to London to work for a major international Swiss bank. Wow, what an exciting opportunity! We had lived in London in the late 80s through my husband's work. This was an opportunity to return to a city we knew and loved.

Consider The Impact Of Career Decisions In The Long Term

There was just one slight problem. My other half started to get cold feet. When it came to decision time, he started to get nervous. "I could quit public accounting (and the ungodly hours) and join one of the supra national institutions in DC," he pleaded. I painfully had to remind him that this was not about him, it was about *me*. I was not asking him to work fewer hours. Inside my stomach was churning. How could I continue to support his career ambitions if he didn't support mine? Wouldn't I always feel short-changed and perhaps even spiteful later in life? I hated the thought of being one of those "could have been" people. I only had one life to live and I wanted to live it to the utmost.

This predicament scared the hell out of me. It felt like our relationship was at a crossroads. Go this way and your marriage will succeed, go that way and your marriage will fail. Or worse yet, either way you decide, your marriage will fail. If we didn't go for this move, how would we feel in five years, ten years or even twenty years? For weeks we discussed the pluses and minuses. I needed to get back to the bank with a final answer. Our discussions were emotionally draining, but we were able to maintain respect for one another throughout.

Change Comes With Uncertainty

We finally agreed that I would take the job. This was not the end of the saga however. Doubt and discussions continued while we waited for my work permit to be approved by the British Immigration Office. The wait was longer than usual due to the recession in the UK and weeks turned into months. As the months passed, we started to think about staying in Virginia. We started looking at houses, which were much more affordable than in the UK. My temporary consulting job was starting to feel more permanent. In fact, I was asked to go permanent. Great, just what I needed – more choices and more confusion. One of the most unsettling feelings is when you don't know where you're going to lay down your roots. Is it here or is it there? In between is not a nice place to be.

The waiting was getting ridiculous. We couldn't stand being stuck in purgatory. We took the decision over one weekend that on the following Monday I would turn down the job if the work permit hadn't come through. We both thought that there was little doubt that once Monday came, the work permit would not yet be approved and our decision to stay in the US would then be final. It felt good to have finally made a decision. We knew what we were going to do. We both woke up Monday morning with a sense of relief that we'd made a decision. Monday afternoon the bank called me. The work permit had come through. I'm not making this story up. It really did happen like that.

Even A Temporary Split Of The Family Is Painful

Okay. Regroup. By the end of Monday we had made a final decision (again). We were moving to London. It wasn't all plain sailing even though we knew where we were moving to. It was downright tough. The family had to split up temporarily. Even though it was temporary, it was still very painful. I hope I never have to live through that experience again. I moved to London in April. The kids stayed with their dad until the end of June. This period was especially trying for my other half. He had to take on the role as the primary caregiver while at the same time try to arrange a transfer to London within his firm. He had to drop the kids off at the nursery and pick them up every day. I understand that on several occasions our two youngsters were the last to be picked up, waiting on the step, with lights off and doors locked, holding the teacher's hand. The nursery was very understanding and forgiving.

While my husband was grappling with being a single parent, I was in London fascinated by the buzz and excitement of the city. It was a whole new world. It was exciting, but at the same time I missed my family tremendously. I yearned to be needed again. I even bought a plant so I could have something to take care of – how pathetic is that? The kids finally joined me in June while my other half stayed in the DC area until September to finish up a number of projects.

Opportunities Don't Always Come In Tandem

Once September came around you would have thought the worst was over. A week before my husband was due to join us in London, my father-in-law had a heart attack. Amazingly, Pop survived that scare with flying colors and our family was reunited in September, a week later than originally planned. Moving to London would have been significantly more strenuous if my other half had to look for a new job. The company transfer did come through in the end, which meant there was one less thing for us to worry about.

This is the kind of stress that many dual-career couples face. Opportunities don't always come in tandem. Had my husband not been able to find work right away, or find the right type of work, he might have had regrets himself. Ironically, the move actually furthered his career. He was able to move out of terribly boring auditing work into an accounting advisory role where he was exposed to businesses from all over Europe, helping them raise finance in the US market. Our marriage didn't fall apart. It flourished, but it felt like a close call. The move wasn't easy for the kids either. They seemed a bit shaken at first, but then quickly assimilated into their new environment, as kids do, once we were settled in our new home in the outskirts of London.

The Combination Of Career & Family Forces Equilibrium

What I've found fascinating about this lifestyle of career and family is that it *forces* equilibrium or balance. Had I not had children and just focused on my work, I would have burnt out and my work would have suffered. Alternatively, had I dedicated all of my time to parenting, I would have felt frustrated and trapped and probably would not have been a very good mother at all. Devoting myself to the dual roles of mother and professional forced me to keep balance at home and at work. At work I couldn't stay in the office for hours and days on end. I had kids at home who were waiting to see me, even *looked forward* to seeing me. I had made a commitment to the childcare provider as well to pick them up by a certain time. The people that look after your children have their own personal lives and interests and do need their own free time, no matter how wonderful your kids are.

At home I couldn't get too worked up about the floor being sticky (from toddlers dropping their apple juice) as I had to spend my time more wisely. I knew that all too soon I'd have to wake up at the crack of dawn to catch a flight or a train. Now was the moment to spend quality time with the kids.

The balance I am describing above actually *increases* your level of effectiveness, productivity and enthusiasm at home and at work. Have you ever worked for a number of hours in deep concentration and then your productivity plummets because you need a break? The career-family existence forces these breaks. For me, having kids saved me from becoming an obsessive individual with the most boring and organized life imaginable. To give you an idea of how obsessive I can be, when my husband thought he'd ask me out for a date, he checked with a few university friends to see what they thought of me. "Brown? She's intense," was the unanimous reply. When I heard this story years later I thought it was harsh, but I do understand how I can sometimes come across in that manner. Once I get involved in something, I tend to go into deep concentration and work at a fierce pace. Oh well, I guess there are worse things to be in life.

Isn't all this change a real drain? Just when you feel you've got things in place, it changes again? That's looking at the glass and seeing it half empty. When you see the glass half full, you realize that if things stayed the same you'd be bored out of your mind and you actually love the fact that there is never a dull moment. You enjoy new surroundings and a new environment. Career and family offers you abundant color in a potentially gray world. Being happy and fulfilled *is* therefore very possible in a career-family lifestyle. It's all about designing it in a unique way that works for *you*.

CHAPTER THREE

Everyone Benefits

YOUR PROFESSION IS BETTER OFF WITH YOU THAN WITHOUT YOU

WHEN A WOMAN CHOOSES CAREER *and* family everyone benefits. Your profession benefits as it hasn't lost you as a valuable, trained and skilled resource post maternity leave. You're an educated woman. You have the drive and energy to make an impact. Staying engaged in whatever profession you're in means that that profession benefits. That sector has a more diverse workforce as a result of you continuing to contribute. The organization you work for better represents its customers, shareholders, and the community it serves.

You are likely to have enhanced multi-tasking and time management skills due to the demands of the balancing act. Your clients benefit as you can now relate to them on another level. You can establish a more personal rapport with them as they are likely to have children as well. And everyone loves to talk about their kids! You can also relate to your team and staff members better. They too have families. Perhaps you're able to understand their behavior at work better as a result. Your role as a parent can reinforce your credibility as a professional, as a manager. You may be more patient and tolerant. You can approach problems with a greater degree of maturity and perspective.

FAMILY LIFE GIVES YOU PERSPECTIVE AND COMPASSION

After a difficult night at home with a young child with a high fever, problems at work don't seem to be such a big deal. You are worried to death about your child's health: is it meningitis; swine flu? All kinds of other ugly possibilities pop into your mind. After such episodes I was always able to go to work with a renewed sense of what was important in life, as well as a renewed sense of confidence that I could take on any challenge my job would throw at me on that day. Difficulties at work paled in comparison to confronting potential illnesses at home.

An executive coach I recently met at a networking event agreed with my assessment of the benefits of women returning to work after childbirth. She recounted the transformation of one of her friends who had a reputation for being a nightmare at work until she had kids. Having kids mellowed her. The rough edges became smoother. She was as hard driving and demanding as ever, but had a more well-balanced manner when dealing with pressing issues.

Two Careers Are Better Than One

When you and your partner both have careers, your partnership benefits. You have mutual appreciation for the parenting as well as breadwinner role. You share in the responsibilities of raising a family as well as providing economic security. According to sociologists, high quality partnerships often result from this type of arrangement. What a difference from my mother's generation where there were very clearly delineated boundaries between the duties of husband and wife. The partnership also benefits from greater economic security as well as flexibility. By flexibility I mean the ability to more easily switch careers or change lifestyles. Perhaps have a break between jobs or take on a lesser paying job as a result of changing professions. Less pressure on the man to bring home the bacon has to be a good thing. This lifestyle choice also gives the father the opportunity (and obligation) to spend more time with the kids. More about how the kids benefit in a moment.

A Career Makes You A Better Partner

Being a professional as well as a mother can make you a better partner/spouse. You know what it's like dealing with the big bad outside world. It's tough. You've experienced the challenges of earning a living – getting that promotion, dealing with internal politics, meeting performance targets and the pressure of deadlines. You are exposed to external issues, are intellectually challenged and have more varied interests – something your partner perhaps finds attractive? You are able to support your partner better because you are fulfilled in your own work. You've had your own rewarding experiences outside of the home. You also have the know-how that allows you to offer sound professional advice, especially if you work in similar fields. As an outsider you can provide a clearer and impartial view on interpersonal or political conflict that your partner is struggling with at work.

One of the biggest benefits I've experienced is that I can really and truly understand when my husband has to work late. I know first-hand how much effort it takes to progress your career. As a result I rarely phone him to ask when he's coming home, unless we have a specific commitment which was agreed in advance. I figure that with all the pressures he already has on him at work, the last thing he needs is more pressure from home. Excellence doesn't always happen between 9am and 5pm.

It wasn't until my mother-in-law was visiting us in London in the late 80s that I realized this wasn't a conventional husband and wife arrangement. When she asked me what time hubby was going to be home, I replied, "I have no idea. I'll know when I hear from him." She thought that was strange, especially since she was visiting. I proceeded to say that I had no intention of calling him, but she was welcome to do so. Does it work in reverse you ask? When I worked in the city, there were times when I called my husband to say I was going to be late, so could he be come to relieve the nanny. He would then worry about me travelling home late on the train (which is reassuring in a way to know someone cares). I don't worry about him in the same way, unless it's going to be *very* late, when all the drunkards tend to travel on the train.

Without a Career, Divorce Is Imminent

I often joke with my husband that I would have divorced him years ago if I hadn't had my own career. I would have wondered how it could possibly take so many hours to do his job. His work in auditing and now in accounting advisory demands long hours. There's no two ways about it, unless you work less than full time. In an accounting advisory role clients sometimes need support at odd hours. Clients are clients and any well-run business has to have a culture of client service. Being a business person myself, I completely understand that clients have problems after 5pm and on the weekends as well. Do I like our weekends interrupted by calls? No, I hate it, but those interruptions are sometimes on account of my work as well, so how could I possibly get mad? Interruptions from cell phone calls and Blackberry messages are the price you pay for being a professional. You just need to keep them in check in the overall scheme of things. Short-term sacrifices often result in long-term gains.

My empathy for my other half's job doesn't stop with the clients' demands. There are also the demands from staff or from colleagues. For some reason colleagues, especially younger, less experienced ones, tend to gravitate to my husband's office on Friday evenings to bring up sticky technical topics or perhaps complex personal situations. Maybe they know he will be there. Maybe they know the office will be in wind-down mode and it's a good time to have a longer conversation (longer conversations are one of my husband's unique talents). I do sometimes get proprietary about Friday nights being eaten up by non-family matters. It's nearly the weekend, for goodness sake. This is our time, family time. Can't your problems wait until Monday? Then the empathy kicks in. I see how rewarding it is for him to coach younger people. He gets a real kick out of it and he's good at it. He reaps huge returns from the investment of time he puts into people. We both laugh about how our neighbors over the years have looked at him suspiciously on account of the odd hours he keeps on Friday nights. "Sure, you were held up in the office alright! Boy, is your wife naïve," they remark (in private).

Career Women Make Bad Mothers

To grab the public's attention, an advertising organization in the UK posted billboard ads which read "Career Women Make Bad Mothers". The point of the campaign was to demonstrate that even in this digital media age, billboards are still an effective means of advertising. It worked, didn't it? It got your attention, right? It certainly grabbed mine. A number of women's groups were outraged by the campaign and the billboards were speedily withdrawn.

Should mothers work? What's best for the kids? This is the wrong question. It's too simple and one dimensional. Children are part of a family unit. When that family unit is strong and healthy, kids do best. This view is backed up by recent research from Columbia University on the impact of working mothers on their children. The study confirmed what *rational* mothers and fathers already knew: it's the relationship we develop with our kids and the happiness of the family that counts the most. This positive effect offsets the potential negative effects on cognitive learning.

Kids benefit from career moms and dads in many ways. Dads tend to be around more as they sometimes are on duty while Mom's at work or travelling. That can't be a bad thing – another parent with a separate source of patience, wisdom and energy. As a career mom you have a bigger tool box of skills to deal with the challenges of childrearing. You also have the confidence and desire to deal with issues head on. That's the style of working you are used to. You have the ability to see the bigger picture and make sure the important things are being addressed. You can monitor your child's progress in school, sports, and social settings and identify where more attention or a different strategy needs to be applied.

"Working parents raise well-balanced children," claims the Editor-in-Chief of fashion magazine *Elle*, Lorraine Candy. "I work in an industry populated with young people, and many of them the proud produce of working mums. They are smart, ambitious, intelligent and grounded. They are inquisitive and engaged with the world. They are above all, super-confident. Many of those I work with cite their parents as role models, especially their working mums."

Mother's Help Is Not Always Best

I would have loved to have been able to tutor my two older kids in English. Given that I was slightly removed from the day-to-day happenings at the school, I was able to see more clearly any gaps in their development. Both kids weren't particularly interested in English and they were getting just average grades. I knew that if they were going to excel academically, especially with the national exams, they would need to improve their English skills. Whatever field they ended up in, English was a crucial foundation. Even though they both recognized that they needed additional support, they wouldn't have entertained the thought of their mother tutoring them. No way, no how! When I tried to get more involved in their schoolwork, they pushed back massively (perfectly normal teenage behavior and a consequence of doing a good job as a parent – they had learned to be independent). For some reason kids are more receptive to a complete stranger's advice than the advice of their own flesh and blood.

I was also able to recognize that each child needed his/her *own* tutor in order to concentrate on the English lessons rather than worrying about sibling rivalry. I was not only able to spot weaknesses (and talent) as a result of my professional life, but was also able to quickly spring into action. You need to recognize in business, and at home, when outside help is best. Don't take it personally. Listen to your logical brain and your emotional brain. Your emotional brain gives you the adrenalin you need to take quick action. Your child's wellbeing is at stake here. Your logical brain allows you to figure out what's best, separate from the emotion.

You have to accept that you personally are not in a position to solve every problem. It can be a hard fact to accept, especially in your role as a mother. Sometimes outsiders can have a positive influence on your child's skills and talents in a manner which you as a parent, by definition cannot. This is another example of why spending 100% of your time with your children isn't necessarily benefiting them or you. If you're not recharging your batteries apart from your children, you can become less enthusiastic, less patient and even potentially burnt out in your role as mother.

Your Professional Skills Enable You To Respond To Family Crises

One of the most difficult parenting moments I ever experienced was when my daughter was preparing for her GCSE exams (standardized tests taken at the age of 16 in the UK). At that stage students are given more freedom to organize themselves and their work, which teaches them independence and prepares them for studies at university. Classes and homework are less structured, encouraging students to think independently. My daughter had psyched herself out that she would never finish all the work that needed to be done on time. The schedule wasn't all laid out for her. She had to lay it out herself, figure out what she had to do when. She wasn't sleeping well, eating well and had lost her confidence. None of my words of comfort or reassurance seemed to help. How could they? I was just an American mom. How could I possibly understand the ins and outs of the English school system? Each night when I returned home from work I would find her depressed and teary-eyed. This was not the young lady I was used to seeing. Where was the energy and confidence that she once exuded? She was not only not eating, not sleeping and emotionally unsettled, but also studying too much.

Worried and feeling desperate, I knew I had to take action. I wrote a confidential letter to the principal of the school to share my concerns. As soon as she received the letter, she called and suggested pairing my daughter up with a mentor. The mentor she recommended was one of the younger teachers who could more easily relate to my daughter and vice versa. She was also a teacher who knew my daughter, but wasn't currently teaching her. Their weekly informal chats were just what the doctor ordered. They chatted about how the week was going, what to expect when for which subject. This young teacher was able to take away the fear of the unknown. My daughter was soon back to her normal self. Without a doubt my career had prepared me for taking the appropriate steps, and taking them swiftly before matters turned for the worse.

Children Learn Teamwork By Watching Parents Work Together

Kids also benefit by seeing how a family works together and how conflict can be resolved without tearing each other's throats out. Managing a busy career and home life involves using a number of skills: teamwork, conflict management and problem solving to name just a few. Kids learn by observing these skills in action. They learn to resolve their own conflicts, with their parents, their siblings and friends, in a positive manner. They may not, on the first attempt, approach a situation in the most effective way. When you as a parent and a spouse demonstrate teamwork and conflict resolution, you become credible in your children's eyes to give advice on how to handle things in the best way. Your actions give you the authority to say, "Look how your dad and I work things out. We don't talk to each other like that." Actions speak louder than words. If on the other hand, you avoid conflict instead of resolving it, and get into big rows where no one communicates, they learn that too.

No Matter What Choices You Make, Your Teenage Kids Will Resent You

What happens when the kids become teenagers? Do you remember those turbulent years? It doesn't matter what choices you make, teenagers will resent you no matter what you choose. You'll never stack up. Dads can sometimes suffer pretty badly at the hands of teenage daughters. For many years every conversation that my daughter started to have with her dad began with the word "no". They were at odds with one another in every dialogue they tried to engage in. One afternoon, my daughter commented to me, "Why do you need Dad?" This gives you an indication of the low point the relationship had reached. This question seemed hurtful. I patiently responded, "It's not about *needing*. It's about companionship and wanting." He challenged her thinking and she resented it, at least for the time being.

This strained relationship between father and daughter caused me a lot of internal grief. I felt like I was being tugged between the two of them, both of them wanting me to defend their side. My husband would get very frustrated that I didn't intervene and set the record straight. My intuition told me that it was best that we played good cop, bad cop so that my daughter felt that she could still come talk to me, otherwise, she would feel completely isolated at home. When my husband shared his anguish about his relationship with our teenage daughter, I often replied, "She will grow out of it.""*When*?" he would yell. It took about five years for this phase to pass, which at the time felt like a lifetime.

Keep A Watchful Eye On Your Teenagers

The point is not whether you work or don't work. The point is that you need to give your kids room to grow and be independent, but at the same time keep a close eye on things and take action when it becomes necessary. Having a career doesn't prevent you from doing this. Indeed, it prepares you very well for dealing with the challenges of teenagers.

Our elder son, like any normal teenage boy, spent an inordinate amount of time on the computer. This was just before the online social networks took off. Online video games were all the rage for young boys. We were concerned about putting a computer in our son's room – if we did that, there would be no way of knowing how much school work he was actually doing. At least this way we knew that if he was in his room, he was either studying or sleeping. So we decided to put the computer on the ground floor in the small family room. This worked well until our son started shutting the door on a regular basis. My husband offered our son two alternatives: he could either keep the door open or he wouldn't have to worry about the door as my husband would remove it from the hinges altogether. The door then magically stayed open.

Next on the agenda was controlling the websites our son was accessing. You've got to give your teenagers some space, but at the same time you can't be naïve about what they could be getting up to. I then thought, "Our head of technology has two sons who are approaching the teenage years. I bet you he's got some ideas." My colleague taught me about "cookies". I could then see which websites had been recently accessed on the computer. I wanted to let our son know that we were watching, not because we didn't trust him, but rather because we cared. One evening I said very casually, "Hey son, do you have a minute, I want to show you something." We sat down together in front of the computer screen as the list of recently accessed sites appeared on the screen: Girls/Girls/Girls, Men and Motors, and your imagination can work out the rest. Although I'm sure he continued to access sites for the remainder of his teenage years I'm confident that this event did have an impact on his behavior and made him think about what he was doing. You're not always going to be around, so it's best to teach your kids the how and why so they can then think on their own.

Don't lose faith. Teenagers do eventually turn into caring and thoughtful adults. At some point they even realize that a lot of the "nonsense" their parents used to do and say now makes a lot of sense. They are actually *thankful* that you taught them independence, that you didn't tolerate bad behavior, and that you set certain standards of conduct. My two twenty plus year old children tell me stories of students they meet who can't organize themselves out of a box, about how people aren't responsible for showing up for meetings that they've agreed to. You'll love that moment. It makes the struggle through the teenage years well worth it. Remember that your decision about career is enduring. Your kids won't be kids forever, but your positive influence as a brilliant career mother lasts a lifetime – from toddler, through the teenage years, well into young adulthood.

WHAT'S IN IT FOR YOU?

If your profession benefits, your relationship with your partner benefits and your kids benefit, how do *you* benefit? You benefit from having a wonderfully varied and balanced life. You cherish your role as a mother. You love being a professional and feeling like you're in demand. You thrive in your role as wife/partner. And the best part is you take great pride in knowing that you are equally effective, competent, happy and full of vigor in each of these roles. It's not a zero sum game: just because you win, it doesn't mean that someone else has to lose. This is why the career-family combination is more like yin and yang. Your various roles feed off of one other. They are synergistic.

If you are eager to have a career, and that, combined with having a family is going to make you feel happy and fulfilled, then that's what you should do. By doing what you want to do, you have a greater chance of being healthy. "Joy is a vitamin," observes Barbara Sher, career counselor and bestselling author. In other words, when you are doing what you love, it stops depression and supports your immune system. This is one of the major benefits for mothers who want to continue to pursue a career. The fulfillment from pursuing a career combined with raising a family allows you to share your zest for life with those around you, whether it be at home or at work.

CHAPTER FOUR

Be True To Yourself

LISTEN TO YOUR INNER VOICE – YOUR CORE VALUES ARE SPEAKING TO YOU

DO YOU KNOW WHAT YOU BELIEVE IN? Do you know what things are important to you? Do you know who you are? What is your standard for personal conduct? This is all getting to the point about values and principles. When you can answer these questions, you have a good sense of who you are - you have a core set of values. It's these values that guide you, especially during difficult times, times that are stressful or times that require important decisions to be made. Values act as a reference point, a benchmark. You refer to them to double check that you are following the right direction for you. The *right* direction is the direction that's consistent with your inner beliefs.

Values Act As A Compass

When you're at a crossroads and you know you are about to make a critical decision that will shape your future, do take a rational approach. Go over the facts and the pros and cons, but *also* listen to your inner voice. What is it telling you? Never underestimate the value of your intuition. Does it feel right; if not, why not? This intuition is giving you a hint about how the decision looks when benchmarked against your core set of values.

Life is a result of a whole series of decisions and actions. The more you follow your inner voice, your core set of principles, the more your life will unfold into a consistent and gratifying picture.

> *Build your life brick upon brick*
> *Live a life of truth*
> *And you will look back on a life of truth*
> *Live a life of fantasy,*
> *And you will look back on delusion.*
> **Deng Ming-Dao, Chinese author and philosopher**

Values help you make the right decisions *for you*, whether they have to do with family, work, friends, politics etc. They act as your compass.

Why Values Matter In The Workplace

When choosing an employer, you need to look at the culture of the organization, the people, and ask yourself whether you fit in. Does the organization believe in the same things that you believe in? If you include this step in your analysis, as well as looking at the hard facts (profitability, growth potential, etc), you are likely to improve the quality of your decision making and choose an employer that you will stay with for a longer period of time.

It's a recipe for disaster if you work for an organization which doesn't display the values that you hold dear. If you believe that everyone should be treated with respect – and it follows that the modus operandi should be an open, transparent working environment – you will be miserable in an organization that has a dictatorial approach and one that makes decisions behind closed doors.

Culture Drives Organizational Behavior

Through a merger and acquisition, I ended up briefly working for an organization that operated in a culture of secrecy. A culture where employees were discouraged from voicing their opinions (they were downright scared!), especially if their views didn't mirror management's view. It was a suffocating environment. I did enjoy some of the new personalities that joined the organization (I really do like change), but then realized that these other cultural issues were eating away at me.

It wasn't until I left the company that I realized what was happening. Time allows you to see things more clearly. I now see that there was a fundamental disconnect between me and the values of the new organization. An organization's culture used to come a poor second to issues such as profitability, market share and management structure, but now is recognized as the *driver* for an organization's behavior. Culture is synonymous with organization's values.

PROFESSIONAL DECISIONS BASED ON PERSONAL REASONS ARE FINAL

When you understand what makes someone tick, you understand their core values. The financial industry is a revolving door. People come and go all of the time. Over the years I've seen people leave their jobs for personal reasons like they want to spend more time with their family or they want to move closer to elderly parents. If they are leaving for personal reasons, and these reasons are completely consistent with their core beliefs, there's no sense in trying to convince them to stay. They've made the right decision for them. No amount of money, job promotions, or fancy new job titles is going to change their mind.

Personality Differences Can Be Reconciled – Differences In Values Cannot

When choosing a spouse or partner, looking at their belief system is one of the key factors in determining compatibility. "What about interests, looks, and personality?" you ask. Yes, I can't deny that these all play a part in your attraction or your decision to choose that partner. However, differences in values are show stoppers. Perhaps you don't recognize this early on in a relationship, but it will raise its ugly head later on, so be aware.

You can reconcile personality differences, but differences in values cannot be reconciled. If they could they wouldn't be values. Values aren't a moving target.

They are a solid, fixed set of standards to which you apply yourself. It's very interesting to look at successful partnerships where the couple has contrasting personalities. Why do opposites attract? Can you imagine what it would be like if both individuals in a relationship were exactly the same – perhaps both extreme extraverts and big talkers who loved being around people? Neither of them would be able to get a word in edgewise. Each of them would be vying for center stage.

Make Sure You Know What Makes Your Partner Tick

What happens when two people become partners and they don't believe in the same things? What happens if they don't have the same views on having children? What if they have different principles on how children should be raised? Are these irreconcilable differences? What if a husband or wife believes that the institution of marriage is a falsehood, while the other believes that marriage is something to covet and work hard at preserving?

Years ago my other half worked for a manager who prided himself on the fact that he didn't believe that marriage was a long-term commitment. He almost bragged about it. Fair enough, each to his own, but why did he get married? The marriage didn't change his view. How does this story end? You bet, divorce within a year. This is an extreme case of how values within a marriage can't be reconciled, but I think it illustrates the point well.

The key message is that when you are choosing a significant other, make sure you understand their fundamental approach to life. What makes them tick?

Values In Schools And Childcare Settings

What other kinds of decisions require going back to your basic set of principles? Choosing childcare and schools for your child require following the same exercise. Consider whether your potential choices are in line with your values. Before my kids went to school, I would have never thought that choosing a school was such a big deal. A school has teachers, teaches kids how to behave, how to read and write... So what's all the fuss? What I have learned is that schools are just like any other type of organization. Each has its own culture, character and set of values, in addition to their academic standing and achievements. Given that each child is unique, choosing a school that matches your child's personality and interests is *essential*. It's also essential that you and your partner's values agree with the values of the school. Values lie at the heart of your child's education.

Stick To Your Guns – That's Integrity!

True happiness also depends on integrity. Your values can't change when circumstances change. Values require you to stick to your guns regardless of the situation. This may sound easy, but in practice it's not, especially when you are outnumbered. There is comfort in the majority. Group think takes over. This is why there is so much talk about diversity in the context of organizational behavior. It's one of the ways to combat group think. Instead of having people of similar age, race, and gender, you want to bring together a group of people with varied backgrounds, who can offer more varied perspectives.

During one of my speeches at a business-network event, I raised this point about integrity. It really seemed to resonate with the predominantly female audience. A few of the women almost had a look of desperation in their eyes, as if to say, "Why doesn't the business world understand that it's incredibly motivating to work for an organization that demonstrates integrity?" Sometimes we forget that of course people work for money, but money's not the only motivating factor. People feel good about working for organizations that demonstrate integrity. It also makes people feel like they are working for a greater good and not just buying time and getting paid.

Do You Lead A Double Life?

If you have a core set of values and you have integrity (you stick to your guns when the going gets tough), doesn't it follow that you have to be you in *all* settings? Do you lead a double life? Are you a different person socially than you are in your professional environment? Do you follow the same set of principles in these two settings? How do you treat your colleagues, your staff, your clients, your suppliers, your spouse/partner, your children or your own parents? Let's say you're considering having a more serious relationship with a guy. How does he treat his mother? Does he show respect? How a man treats his mother will be a good indication of how he will treat you. That's not to say you are in the least bit like his mother, but it is to say that it reflects the value that he places on close relationships, which will carry over to your relationship.

The news during this past year has been packed with stories about scandals. You name it, it's been done. It's made me wonder how these individuals (they are really criminals, even though their crimes are more clever), behaved at home. And remember, these scandals haven't just happened in the financial world. Yes, you have the likes of Bernie Madoff and dozens of other financial scandals, but these shenanigans have also happened in the sports world, for example. England's Harlequin rugby team faked a blood injury; rugby is supposed to be a *gentleman's* game. Then there's the boss of the Renault team at last year's Singapore Grand Prix conspiring with its driver to cause a deliberate crash in order to fix the results of the race. Did these offenders promote this type of behavior in their own kids? Do they teach their kids to cheat at school?

How Do You Know It's The Right Thing To Do?

Is there any way to test out a decision to see if it's really the "right" thing to do? One useful tip is to ask yourself how the public would react to the story of a particular action if it were plastered all over the front page of a newspaper. It doesn't matter whether a particular action was legal or not. The public looks beyond legality. It's how it would be *perceived* by the public which is important. If you have to do a lot of explaining, it's likely not to be the right decision. The circumstances look a bit murky and that's why you're struggling to justify your actions.

Here's another tip. Try this one in an important meeting where everyone's completely lost their senses about what the right thing to do is. Ask, "What would your mother say?"or "What would your father do?" This yanks people back to their basic principles as it's in the home, not in business school, where values are learned. It's a pretty powerful tool, especially when you're surrounded by yes men or colleagues who can't separate the logic from their own personal interests.

The UK Parliament's expenses scandal demonstrates this point beautifully. This is the kind of test that would have raised the red flag in the UK Parliament had someone asked the question whether the accepted practice for reimbursing expenses was reasonable? It would have come to light that the *spirit of the law* – compensating ministers for their *hardship* of living in London while maintaining their primary residence – had been violated. What would my mother think is reasonable for me to claim as an expense? Should I refurbish my duck pond for £5,000 and ask for reimbursement? I think not.

Being True To Yourself Is A Magnet For Solid Relationships

Being true to yourself, following your own set of values and principles has a positive side effect. You become a magnet for building solid relationships. Haven't you also found it easier to relate and deal with people who you can count on behaving in a certain way? Friends or colleagues whose behavior is all over the place are taxing to deal with. You never know who's going to respond: Dr Jekyll or Mr Hyde. One day they will react one way, and the next day they react in a completely different way to the same set of circumstances. These types of people are very high maintenance. They wear you out. You can't count on them to behave in a consistent manner. When you are consistent in your own behavior, it makes it easier for others to relate and understand you.

Inconsistency Breeds Mistrust

In a professional setting you lose trust and faith in your manager or organization when they don't demonstrate consistency. Inconsistency breeds mistrust. I have seen this happen in business, especially when there have been frequent management changes. Employees start feeling like the company doesn't have a consistent set of values. In fact each new management team professes the *new* philosophy, which of course is much better than the old one. The new management team has been enlightened. Unlike the prior management, the new management has the *right* strategy. When employees lose trust, it's almost impossible to galvanize them into following a new way forward. They've already made up their mind that this is just another management whim, soon to be changed by the next management team and the next culture that follows.

Consistent Behavior Is A Powerful Tool For Managing A Business

On the other hand, if a business can demonstrate a consistent approach, it can be a very powerful quality. Businesses that follow a consistent philosophy are more likely to have employees who are moving in the same direction as the management strategy. The employees trust that the organization will follow a well-established and well-articulated path. Customers also understand and trust companies which behave in a predictable way.

As a loyal Honda customer, I trust that Honda values quality and reliability and will follow through if I have any maintenance issues with any of my cars. I also know that they truly value customer feedback. They solicit opinion about their performance at all levels of the company, whether it be the local dealership or the holding company (checking up on the service provided by the local dealership).

Using this philosophy when dealing with people one-on-one is equally effective. One of the ways I was able to gain respect from senior managers, especially when I had to deal with sensitive matters such as reviewing expense reimbursements, was to follow a *consistent* set of principles – principles that seemed fair and dovetailed with my own value system. This allowed me to stick to my guns under pressure. I would handle expense discrepancies carefully and ensured that, although straightforward in my style, I kept matters confidential. I would schedule meetings with the managers in their offices to discuss the concerns I had about their expense claims, where claims for dinners or lunches included exorbitant bottles of wine. They were uncomfortable situations, but most of the time the issues were resolved amicably, and claims were dutifully revised and resubmitted.

Happiness Is Predicated On Being The Real You

If you know who you are and what you believe in, and you follow through on those beliefs, at home *and* at work, you can achieve harmony, be happy. Happiness isn't only about having the opportunity to enjoy the rewards of both career and family, it's also about being the *real you* in both worlds. The career-family lifestyle is fast moving. Quick decisions will need to be made. Your integrity will be tested. As long as you are following your core set of values when making those decisions, you will find your way. Being true to yourself is one of the keys to happiness.

CHAPTER FIVE

It's All About The Team

INVEST IN YOUR TEAM, YOUR KEY RELATIONSHIPS

Couples That Play Together Stay Together

WITHOUT THE TEAM, balancing career and family doesn't work. End of story. You simply cannot do it all and it's no fun doing everything yourself anyway. The answer to the question, "How do you do it all?" should be, "The team makes it happen." This is why you need to invest in your team, in your key relationships. Let's start with your significant other. Amidst all of the chaos and time pressures, you need to make one-on-one time for your partner. Spending time together allows you to grow together. Couples that play together, stay together. Find that common interest outside of the children which you can enjoy together.

It can really be tough to find quiet moments when the two of you can actually have a conversation. That's why you've got to make special time for just the two of you. Back when we had all of our kids at home and a full-time nanny, my husband would sometimes come home early and be under the false belief that he and I were actually going to have a conversation. No chance. Each of the three kids wanted attention. I also needed to check in with the nanny and make sure things were on track. If I sensed this wasn't the case, I would suggest slight changes, perhaps highlighting that homework was non-negotiable: no computer games until the work was done no matter what the kids promised. In the end my husband would give up in desperation and let out a sigh, "I guess I'll talk to you once the kids go to bed and the nanny's left for the day."

Tennis was our "us time". Our daughter took up the game and was getting so good at it that we decided we needed take lessons to keep up the pace, otherwise, she'd soon be beating us. We didn't want her to feel like she was playing with two uncoordinated idiots. She has now put the game on the back burner due to her studies, but we are still playing strong. Having a common interest and spending time together allows us to relate to one another as individuals, like it was in the beginning of our relationship without the kids.

Another handy tip is to plan dates and/or short honeymoons: an occasional dinner out on the weekend is a real treat or a long weekend at a nice resort or hotel. It brings you back to basics and you remember what brought you both together in the first place. Once the kids leave it will be just the two of you again, so it's good practice for the future. It will also make the transition from a house full of kids to an empty nest easier.

Your Relationship As A Parent Lasts A Lifetime

The next most important relationship to invest in is the one with your kids. The job of a parent lasts a lifetime, way past maternity leave. I have chatted with some new moms who naturally focus heavily on the time they spend with their kids during and right after maternity leave. One mom was sharing her grief about how her daughter would cry every morning when she'd drop her off at daycare. I tried to lift her spirits. "They get over it, trust me," I said. "As soon as you're out of sight they get on with their day and have a great time." Kids learn at an early age how to hit your hot buttons. Your relationship with your nine year old or your teenager is no less important than with your toddler.

One-on-One Time Makes Kids Feel Special

Again I make the point that quality time is not a myth, or some fantasy to relieve parents' guilt about not spending enough time with their kids. Quality time fuels quality relationships. It's worth giving some thought to how you spend time with your kids in their various stages. The way they like to spend time now will be very different to how they will want to spend time when they're older. One-on-one time is also very effective with kids. It makes them feel important. Kids act differently in a one-on-one situation with a parent than they do when siblings are around. The sibling dynamics of competition and jealousy fall away. You see that child for who he or she really is and they tend to open up more, reveal what's going on in their heads.

The teenage years are a tough time for kids and parents. Teenagers challenging parents is part of the natural process of growing up. You will take it personally, but you shouldn't. The one-on-one approach worked well for us when our kids went through those confusing and trying times. My other half took up golf lessons with our son. Saturday mornings was their time. He wasn't a great fan of golf, but because our son was interested he thought he would try it. Our son on the other hand was a natural. He relaxed and could hit some very nice shots. His dad's golf skills, well, let's just say there was room for improvement. Our son relished the idea that there was something he was better at than his dad. From his dad's perspective, it didn't matter. Learning how to play golf wasn't the main objective.

Develop Mutual Respect
For Your Childcare Provider

Consider your relationship with your childcare provider to be one of the cornerstones of career-family success. It's the linchpin of the career-family combination, especially in the early years. Given the vital role the childcare provider plays in your child's life, wouldn't you want to ensure a strong, healthy relationship?

Make the childcare provider feel like an important part of the family unit - because that's what she is. This means treating her with respect, but also setting the same high expectations for her that you would set for your own family members. If she believes she is just an employee or an impersonal third party service, then she'll feel no guilt in calling in sick with the slightest sniffle. It's a two-way street, and if you have an understanding that that is the case and you operate as a team, you will find that the childcare provider strives to meet this standard.

In the later years when we could afford live-in nannies, I tried to instill this philosophy of mutual respect and mutual responsibility. Treat others like you want to be treated. I made it clear that I had no problem with vacation days and time off – in fact I encouraged this – but suggested that the nanny's schedule mimic our vacation plans as much as possible. When that wasn't possible, we had an understanding that the nanny was responsible for finding appropriate cover. This saved a lot of headaches. Most of the time the nanny had friends who could fill in for her. Her friends usually already knew the kids as well, which made the transition easier.

Develop Continuity Between You & Your Childcare Provider

Here's another great story about Aggie, whom I mentioned earlier, who looked after our kids when I was in graduate school. One night when I came from school to pick up the kids, Aggie said that she had just grilled some Persian yogurt chicken (she was originally from Iran) and invited the three of us to dinner. Wow! What an offer! That meant I didn't have to go home and cook fish fingers for the fifth night running. It was such a welcome break from the routine, and it gave us a chance to just talk, like adults. When you drop off and pick up your kids from childcare, there is often not much of a chance to have a chat. It's all rush, rush. At the end of the evening, Aggie said to me that in all of her years of looking after children, she never felt more like part of a team than she did with our family. Where our family started and hers began was sometimes blurred. Her two teenage sons were also part of the team. They often babysat for us on the weekend. Finding this kind of continuity for our kids, especially when I was under so much pressure at school and my other half was under so much pressure at work, was a godsend.

The Parent-School Partnership

Your child's school is the other critical relationship in your personal world that you need to attend to. Consider the school and you as a parent to be a partnership. Some schools will emphasize this and put it into practice as well. The way I look at it is you need to keep up your end of the bargain. This way, if your child runs into some sort of trouble, the school is there to support you. It's the two-way street theme again. Also, keep your eye on the ball. How is your child doing in school? Do they seem happy? Are you getting regular feedback? There's nothing worse than learning about an issue that has been going on for a while, rather than at the beginning when it's easier to turn things around. Where possible show your commitment to the school at fundraising events and other activities. You'll get a return on your investment tenfold.

YOU WORK FOR PEOPLE, NOT ORGANIZATIONS

Time to move on to the professional environment. Do the same principles apply? Yes, of course they do. At the end of the day you work for people, not for companies or organizations. It's all about the people you work with and for as well as the people that work for you (your career progress makes this inevitable - if no one works for you at the moment, they will do in the future, I'm sure). Investing in relationships at work makes work worthwhile, makes it fun. Yes, money is important, but job satisfaction is also closely correlated to how much you enjoy your interpersonal relationships at your work. Do you enjoy spending time with the people around you?

Successful Teams Include Spiritual Leaders & Task Leaders

You may have learned at university that teams have two dimensions: people orientation and task orientation. Teams need both qualities to succeed. The spiritual leader (oriented towards people) usually provides the high-level direction and gets the team pumped up and motivated. The task-oriented members see the detailed steps that need to be taken in order to make the project a reality. What needs to happen when and by whom? The team will fail if you don't have both of these dimensions. The two qualities of people orientation and task orientation actually feed off of one another. They keep the team in motion.

A former manager and now good friend was one of the best spiritual leaders I've ever worked for. He made work fun and as a result our group was a coherent team, although each of us individually had our unique strengths. He set a high standard for performance. A strong work ethic and having fun can go hand in hand. In a trading room everyone's under enormous pressure to perform. Laughter and humor is a great way to cope.

The team used to tease me about wearing white socks and sneakers on the way to work. "It was so American," I was told. I thought it was practical - no sense in getting my nice leather shoes wet in the unending London drizzle. One Friday evening as I changed into my sneakers, I looked under my desk to grab my white socks, but they were nowhere to be found. "How could they disappear? Could someone have stolen them?" I wondered. Monday morning came and I received an internal envelope. What do you know? It contained one sock. Later that afternoon, another internal envelope arrived. Yup, sock number two. This continued for days. I'm glad I was able to provide some humor for the team. It was pretty funny. Seventeen years later the team still keeps in touch, with our former manager still keeping the connections alive. Now that's a team.

The Team Benefits When You Reach For The Stars

If it's all about the team, does that mean I should give up my own goals and aspirations so that the rest of the team can succeed? It's similar to the family unit. Giving up who you are within the team is not in the team's best interest. Consider which of your goals are the critical ones and stick to those. Work with the team to incorporate those goals. The team will be better off because of it. Allow yourself to accommodate and compromise when it comes to the less important goals. Following your dreams makes you a *positive* person, rather than a selfish one, as long as you work with others to make your dream happen.

Reaching for the stars makes you a *better* team member. When you follow your own dreams, you are a better role model and coach. No sense in coaching others to develop and set goals if you yourself haven't done just that: set yourself high aspirations. Going after your own dreams gives you the necessary experience to make you an effective and credible coach. Having fed your own ambition, you are able to continue to support and encourage ambition in others.

Teamwork Doesn't Mean 50/50

Teamwork doesn't necessarily mean splitting up each individual task or responsibility 50/50. I would argue that there are economies of scale when you agree on areas of specialization. Even with specialization, you need to have the understanding that you may be called on to cover your team member's area. This sounds like a very business-like concept, and maybe it was developed there, but it works equally well at home. Responsibilities are best divided according to skill set and/or preference. This doesn't necessarily have to be explicitly agreed in the beginning, unlike a work environment. It can develop as a natural process as long as both team members feel like each of them is making a significant contribution. Working together over time you can find equilibrium.

Early in my marriage I was determined to learn how to cook. I loved to eat and appreciated the impact good food would have on my health. As a high energy person, my body demanded a lot of good quality food. Without it, I would get headaches, lose concentration and be in a really foul mood. So I set out to buy a few cookbooks I could afford to get started with. By contrast, I hated doing the administrative paper work associated with running a household: the bills, forms and taxes. In those early days, my husband and I would end up paying the same bills twice. One evening I exclaimed in frustration, "I would be happy if I never wrote another check in my life!" We found a happy sub-division of labor: I cook, he does the paperwork. We both consider it a fair trade.

When you're balancing work and family it's inevitable that you will need to fill in for each other at some point. Your specialization might be preparing the family meal, but then who cooks when you're travelling? Although you won't particularly enjoy the responsibility you've picked up, or vice versa for your partner, there's a positive side effect. Each of you ends up appreciating the contribution that the other one makes to the team. You're not taken for granted and you don't take your partner for granted.

SUPPORT THE DEVELOPMENT OF YOUR TEAM MEMBERS

You're The Team Leader At Work

If you are part of team, it means that you have a duty to support the development of each team member. In your work environment, nourish the ambition of your team members, direct reports and other key relationships. Provide *guidance* – don't do it all yourself. Give your team members the space they need to develop on their own. At work, my philosophy has been that you should take all of your allocated vacation days. If you don't, that's a poor reflection on you and your lack of time management and delegation skills. You won't get brownie points from me for skipping your vacation. This is the old, macho way of thinking. In with the new, out with the old.

When I had a team working for me, I left for vacation knowing that our clients were in good hands and if there was a real emergency, they would call me. What I discovered is that my vacations offered the other team members a fantastic learning opportunity. They were exposed to issues that they wouldn't normally be. They dealt with people (my bosses) they normally wouldn't deal with. It was scary for me and scary for my team at first to let go, but on returning from vacation I always found a stronger team with a renewed sense of confidence.

You're The Parent On The Team

As a parent, supporting the development of your child seems like a no brainer. It's not as easy as it sounds. You will need to give this area constant attention and take action at various stages. You'll want to encourage your kids to try new things. They will resist as they, like many adults, will be afraid of change and the unknown. You will need to teach them that you only fail when you do not try.

Years ago our daughter was a member of the town's gym club and had excelled in the skills that the club taught her. The problem was that the club's coaching resources were limited and she wasn't being pushed to her ability. When we suggested switching to another club, she strongly resisted and was tearful for several nights running as we tried to come to a mutual decision. After several days of distressing conversations, she did finally agree to switch clubs. It wasn't until several years later that she herself recognized that she was being held back at the other club. You want your kids to make their own decisions within reason, but at the same time you have more life experience to fully assess the situation. It works best when you let your kids make the final decision, but make sure you've shared with them all your relevant life experience.

You Are Your Partner's Biggest Fan

In a dual-career family, it's often the case that each partner is each other's most trusted advisor. Each is respected for his or her business acumen, professional knowledge and experience. You are therefore your partner's biggest fan. You help him think through obstacles at work and brainstorm about potential solutions. The crucial difference between your advice and the advice from other advisors is that you can be trusted. You have no ulterior motives. You're not in competition for the same role or position. What you're interested in most is ensuring that your partner enjoys his career and is able to pursue his ambitions.

My husband and I often talk about work and business at home. Our kids get fed up with all the "blah, blah and blah" as they call it. It's so rewarding to be able to exchange views and see issues from a completely unexpected angle. We each have our own strengths and weaknesses, which tend to be complementary. This is why the advisory role of a partner is so valuable. What you see, your partner can't see and vice versa.

You're The Childcare Provider's Boss Or Client

Just when you thought perhaps you were too young to be a boss or an important client. Think about it: when you hire a childcare provider, you are the boss or the client. In any case, you're in the driving seat to help this important team member get the most out of her role. Get to know what her longer-term goals are and think about how you could help her in achieving those goals.

Let's say you take your child to the provider's home. She, like any other member of your team will only be receptive to your support if your relationship is already on steady ground. How do you get it on steady ground? Your actions need to demonstrate that you recognize the provider's value and contribution to the team. Show your respect by being punctual and reliable. Communicate concerns and address them promptly, showing that you do care about how she is coping.

Support The Childcare Provider's Authority

Support the childcare provider's authority. Your kids understand through your words and your actions that the provider is the boss when you or the dad is not around. As with your partner, don't disagree with the provider on issues affecting the kids in front of them; have sensitive discussions *in private* to resolve any differences. Show support of the decisions she has taken in your absence. Beware of *arbitrage*! Kids are highly skilled arbitrageurs. Frequently used phrases include, "My mom says I can do my homework later. My mom says I can have dessert every night, even when I don't finish my dinner." Be a united front, a wall. You will also need to be a united front with your partner. Kids are highly skilled in arbitraging between parents as well.

GET BUY-IN FROM THE TEAM

There's no doubt about it. It takes longer when you consult with others before making a decision than it does when you make the decision on your own. If you're part of a team, however, you expect to be consulted about any major decisions. Show your team respect by getting buy-in from them for any meaningful decisions, especially if they will have a direct impact on them.

Building Consensus Results In Higher Performance

In a work setting, when hiring a new member of the team involve the other team members in the interviewing process. They're the ones, after all, who will need to work with the new member. The *Pret A Manger* sandwich chain puts this principle into practice. Each candidate is interviewed by all of the team members and the team decides who gets hired. It creates real camaraderie and a sense of control of one's destiny, resulting in high levels of customer service. Without buy-in, the team will be a collection of individuals, each with his or her own agenda.

Kids Support Decisions
When They've Been Involved

In your personal life, hiring a childcare provider will be a colossal decision. As such, it's imperative that you involve all of your personal team members: your partner, your children, or other childcare providers who may be part of the overall arrangement. With nearly twenty five years of experience in combining career and family, I've interviewed a lot of childcare providers. I practice what I preach – everyone gets to vote. Involving your kids in this kind of decision makes them *own* the situation. They can't blame you for hiring the childcare provider. It was a joint decision. They therefore have a vested interest in trying to make the situation work.

I would also recommend that when your kids reach school age, you solicit their feedback about the schools you are considering. A visit with them to the schools is always a good idea. You get a real sense for the place and how your child fits in through these personal visits, something that can't really be done by just reading the prospectus. Ask them which ones they liked, disliked and why. Don't give kids the leeway to say, "You decided which school I had to go to, so it's your fault that I'm unhappy." They need to own whatever the decision is, and play an active role in making the decision result in a successful outcome.

CHAPTER SIX

Organized Chaos

THE DOUBLE WHAMMY OF CAREER AND FAMILY MAKES YOU A MASTER OF TIME EFFICIENCY

Pursuing the dual track of work and family will make you a master of time efficiency. It's inevitable. The intense, but exciting and interesting life that you lead demands you be a good time manager. Being efficient with your time allows you to get more out of life – more variety, more activities and interests, more time for what you *have* to do and more time for what you *want* to do.

You love life! There's so much to learn and do. Sign yourself up for that course or join that club you've been thinking about. You'll find that the things you like to do will crowd out the less important things and that's how it should be. This doesn't mean you'll feel like there is enough time. Sorry to have to break the bad news: there is *never* enough time, no matter how efficient you are, but that's because you have a desire to take advantage of what life has to offer. If you had few interests, a dull family life, few friends, you'd have plenty of time on your hands.

Planning Makes Things Possible

My goal in life was not to become a master of time efficiency. It doesn't sound very glamorous, but it happened as a matter of course. I remember my graduation party (post MBA studies) when my sister was astounded how I was able to host a party for thirty guests without any help. As I was the graduate, I couldn't skip the ceremony, so all the preparation for the party had to be done several days in advance. I had every detail and eventuality covered.

The plan was that when the small group of family returned back to the house after the ceremony, the other guests would be arriving simultaneously. At that moment I would open the fridge (presto, presto) and lay out the platters on the tables. It would be as if a caterer had prepared the tables and delivered the food (which definitely wasn't within my budget at the time). That's just what you do when you have to be in two places at the same time – you organize things in advance. It's no big deal. I think being well organized comes as second nature once you've had a bit of experience.

If You Need Something Done, Ask The Busiest Person

Have you ever heard the expression, "if you need to get something done, ask the busiest person?" It's so true, and as true in a professional environment as it is in one's personal life. One of the reasons for this phenomenon is that the busiest person is also the one who knows how to get things done. He or she knows how to get the right resources, how to organize a team and then how to execute the plan.

The Go-To Person Is Always Busy

In the workplace individuals develop reputations for being the go-to person for specific areas. Their reputation develops as a result of producing consistently high quality work. They then become very busy all of the time. Word of mouth quickly spreads throughout the organization about their competence (good news can travel fast too). When starting a new job, you learn who has the official responsibility for certain functions. You will then hear on the quiet who you really should go to for help.

I discovered this phenomenon when I started my new sales and marketing job in the early 90s. I had to liaise with many different departments, such as Corporate Communications, Compliance, and Legal. When I asked colleagues in my department who I should speak to within these other departments, it often was not the person who was most senior or in charge. They shared with me the inside scoop: "Thomas is in charge of Compliance, but if you want to get a quick commercially-oriented answer, you should go to William." And so it went for almost every department. It was a real eye opener as a young person to see how the real world worked in such stark terms. Always find out who is the go-to person to get the job done. This will save you a lot of time.

Your Lifestyle Has Trained You To Get Things Done

Even though you have a busy lifestyle juggling career and family, you may find that surprisingly you are the one who volunteers at the school for a given project or hosts the neighborhood parties. How can that be? Shouldn't you be the last person on the list to volunteer to get involved?

This is the irony. Because you know how to juggle and organize, you can do more, not only at work but also in your personal life. You have the experience and skills that allow you to get things done.

One summer our elder son suggested that we host a karaoke party for the neighborhood. What a wonderful idea! But where were we going to find the time to organize it? Surely we were not the ones with a lot of time on our hands with two demanding jobs in the city. Never mind. I jumped at the idea and figured I could apply my professional skills to the task to pull it together, which would include building a team. Our son identified a disc jockey and whipped up fancy invitations on his laptop. Our daughter bought the supplies and helped organize the food. Her boyfriend borrowed grills for the BBQ from the school. Neighbors brought chairs. Hubby did the grilling (and most of the worrying before the event). It was a true team effort and a real hoot on the night as we watched neighbors singing their hearts out to Black Eyed Peas' hit song "Where is the Love?"

BEING WELL ORGANIZED REINFORCES TEAM DYNAMICS

To be well organized means that you need to rely on a team. In fact it reinforces the team dynamics. Asking for help should not be seen as a sign of weakness. Have you ever had a boss who does everything him or herself? You feel like a spare wheel. You don't feel like an integral part of the team. What's the point? Why are you there?

Having It All Doesn't Mean Doing It All

Having it all, doesn't mean doing it all. In fact, this is probably the most common mistake women make when trying to combine career and family. What's the point of working so hard if you end up exhausted, stressed and unhappy? This is where you need to ensure your rational, logical voice is heard, especially in the home environment. You must delegate, delegate, and delegate. Don't be afraid to ask for help. You can't physically do it all; there aren't enough hours in the day. A mother who also has a professional career has often been referred to as "Superwoman". This sets a pretty high standard for any woman who wants to follow a similar path. I say, "Step aside Superwoman! Career and family is for *any* woman." *You* can make it work by following the simple, practical steps I cover in this book.

Kids Learn By Doing

The other benefit of delegating and involving other team members is that the other team members *learn*, especially kids. They learn by watching you in action. They see how you approach life in a positive manner and how you involve others to complete projects. This is a skill which will obviously serve them well in the future. It's always better to teach kids how to fish, rather than just giving them the fish.

One evening I came home from a twelve-hour work day to find my elder son lying on the couch watching television. He was on his summer break, and a break he was certainly enjoying. As I walked into the living room he greeted me with, "Mom, when are you going to call Sky and upgrade our service so we can watch more channels?" I felt like *exploding*. How dare he ask me this, having just come home from a grueling day at work, while he relaxed in the comfortable living room that I provided for him? Stay calm. I then replied, "Great idea. Can you call Sky tomorrow and get that set up?"

I went on to remind him that he was part of a team – the family – and had to do his part in running the household. The next evening I had a real sense of accomplishment when I heard him speaking to the customer service department at Sky. He did beautifully, explaining in much clearer detail than I ever could, the various screens he had logged onto to get the additional channels set up. Pretty impressive for a seventeen year old. This is one of many experiences which taught him how to get things done (without the intervention from Mom or Dad).

Organize the Team To Do What They Do Best

The more team members who pitch in, the easier the task at hand becomes (with the proviso that you've organized properly who's doing what). You can see in your head exactly what needs to be done when, but you must recognize the downside of doing it all yourself – the lack of fulfillment of the other team members as well as your own exhaustion. In both the work and home environments think about who is best placed to complete which part of the task. In my home my husband is a fantastic team player, but when it comes to working out the logistics for the family, he leaves it up to me. I find it easier. He's happy to follow my lead (and makes sure I keep my bossiness under control).

You May Work Out The Logistics, But You Need The Team To Implement

Here's an example of a logistics issue in the home environment which required a team effort to resolve. Although most of my graduate classes were from 4 - 6pm, there was one class that I was particularly keen on taking which was only available at 8pm. It was a marketing class that other students had highly recommended. Hubby was fully onboard with the idea, but realistically there was no way he could commit to being home on time for me to catch the train into the city campus.

So the plan was I'd drive the car into the city with the two kids (then aged one and four) in their pajamas, fully fed and bathed. I'd swing by Hubby's office at

7.45pm to pick him up. He'd then drop me off at the campus, and drive the car back home with the kids. It sounds complicated, but it worked perfectly. I made every class, and on time. The kids enjoyed the "outing". My daughter used to wear pink tights to keep her legs warm underneath her nightgown. She said her brain felt like she was going to ballet lessons. So sweet! I could not have done this without everyone pitching in. Mentally I felt I had support from the *whole* family to make this class happen.

PRIORITIZE, RE-PRIORITIZE AND THEN PRIORITIZE AGAIN!

Constantly prioritize what you should be focusing on. The combination of career and family is dynamic, continually moving, so the priorities must move along with it, to maintain equilibrium. Always try to prioritize people over tasks, especially family, although we all know that there are certain mundane tasks, like paying bills and filling out forms, which have to be done to keep businesses and households running. Because there are so many demands on your time, be picky. Spend time on the most important priorities. Take a hard look at the remainder of the demands and consider whether anything should be crossed off the list. Be vigilant about not spending time on silly things, and take it off the list if there's any doubt about its importance. You could always go back later and add it back on if necessary.

Work Hard, Play Hard

When deciding on your priorities, be sure to make personal time. The harder you work, the more critical this point becomes. The expression "work hard, play hard" certainly applies here. A former boss once said to me that she used to work every weekend. She noticed that she was starting to lose her enthusiasm for the job, so she decided to be disciplined about *not* working on weekends. This new found freedom inspired her to join the local tennis club and social theatre group. To her amazement she found that she was able to achieve the same amount in *less* time as she became more creative and efficient at work. After a restful weekend completely detached from work, she was ready to literally jump out of bed on Monday mornings eager to start a new work week. While this formula may not work every single weekend – there may be exceptional circumstances where a hard deadline needs to be met and weekend time has to be sacrificed – most of the time it does work.

I have also seen colleagues who were all about work eventually burn out. They were no longer able to continue with their demanding jobs because they didn't recharge their batteries over the weekend. "Always leave enough time in your life to do something that makes you happy, satisfied even joyous. That has more of an effect on economic well-being than any other single factor," says Paul Hawkens, author, environmentalist and entrepreneur. Life requires you to pace yourself. If you pace yourself and maintain a good mix of work and fun, you'll be in the race longer. Be creative on how you make time for you.

Don't Spend Time On Silly Things

In the professional world a good example of spending time on silly things is poorly organized meetings. How many meetings have you been in where you think, "This is a complete waste of time! Is this meeting really necessary?" Poorly organized and poorly run meetings waste valuable time. Meetings should have a clear objective. At the end of the meeting there should be a conclusion with well-articulated action steps: who is responsible for doing what, by when. By having a clear agenda, sticking to it, and distributing a summary of the meeting (which holds individuals accountable for action points) you can make meetings very productive. If you're invited to meetings which are not obligatory, and you know they are not going to be productive, don't go. Conducting well-organized meetings allows organizations to focus on the fundamentals of delivering products and services, and meeting targets, rather than having meetings for meetings' sake.

In a personal context the same concept applies. When you're disorganized, you waste valuable time. Planning, like planning an agenda, can help enormously. I love to cook, but hate to clean up. I also hate to shop. Cleaning up and shopping for me is spending time on silly things. With the introduction of online shopping I have been able to free up several hours per weekend – and you know how precious several hours on a weekend can be. By planning menus and shopping online, I gain time. To achieve economies of scale, I actually plan several weeks' worth of menus at a time. You know how once you get into something, it's easier to crank it out. Well that's what I found with menu planning.

Saving time by planning doesn't end there. How do you get around reducing the amount of pots and pans that need to be cleaned up? (Washing dishes isn't exactly spending time wisely, unless of course you find it therapeutic.) The answer is to cook more than one meal at a time. I never cook a meal that is just for one sitting. I always at least double the recipe to maximize its value – you get to eat it at least twice. Doubling the recipe doesn't take any more effort. Leftovers get a bad rap, but food can actually taste *better* the second time than the first time. It's like marinating. The flavors really get a chance to seep into the food. I try to cook, or at least prepare, three separate dishes for the week – making six meals – when I do cook. Preparing allows you to do all the cutting and perhaps browning before it's then thoroughly cooked later in the week. Not only does this approach save time, you end up washing fewer dishes. Think about how you might be able to apply this concept of economies of scale to your own personal and professional life so you can create time.

Don't Be Afraid To Ask For Help

Once you've taken a hard look at your list, crossed off the silly things, yet the list still looks too long, what do you do? Think about what could be done by the other team members: your other half, the kids. Have you leveraged their abilities and talents? If there still isn't enough resource, which certainly could be the case, especially if the kids are still young, think about getting outside help. Could a friend or neighbor help in exchange for something you'd be glad to help them out with? Consider asking grandparents to help or pay for outside help – it will be worth every cent in terms of stress relief. And just like the cost of childcare, the cost of other domestic help will be a smaller percentage of your overall salary as you progress in your career.

The good news about time management is that it's a global trend. People today are busy people and businesses are cottoning on to this fact. As a result, more and more products and services are being developed (with the help of technology) which make your personal life and work life easier to manage. In the book *Women Want More: How to Capture Your Share of the World's Largest, Fastest Growing Market,"* Michael Silverstein and Kate Sayre highlight that women want more time and control over their lives. Women want products and services that free up their time, and conversely dislike those that take up time. Retail businesses understand that this is a growing trend rather than a passing fad. More help is on the way.

CHAPTER SEVEN

Follow The Three Cs: The First C Is Commitment

WHAT ARE SOME OF THE OTHER QUALITIES needed to successfully combine career and family? So far we've talked about getting the balance right for *you*, how everyone can benefit, being true to yourself, being well organized and teamwork. I'd like to now introduce the Three Cs: Commitment, Communication and Conflict Management. I've dedicated a chapter to each, given how critical they are in creating a synergistic relationship between work and family life. Let's turn to the most important C first: Commitment.

SUCCESS BEGINS IN YOUR MIND

Commitment is a frame of mind and a prerequisite before you start anything in which you want to be successful. If you're not *committed* to being successful at balancing work and family, forget about it. Don't read any further. It's just not going to happen unless you decide before you even start that it's possible and you *are* going to achieve it. No ifs, ands or buts. Success begins in your mind. I'm not a Neurolinguistic Programming coach, but I have read Paul McKenna's book *Instant Confidence* and absolutely concur that you've got to *believe* in success in order to make it happen.

Believing that you can achieve balance in your life, when at times there seem to be irreconcilable and competing demands, is critical to achieving that balance. I am no Superwoman, nor some brain child, but when I *commit* to something I stick by it come hell or high water. Some people call it being stubborn. Others call it being tenacious. So if *I* can do it, you can too. You will also benefit from a more accommodating and accepting environment for the career-family lifestyle. I'm sure as a bright young woman you have tasted success in either your university studies or your career. What did it take for you to achieve that success? Without a doubt, commitment was one of the major reasons you succeeded. This is no different from the attribute you need for career-family success.

Successful Businesses Are Committed To Their Customers

Success requires commitment regardless of whether it's in the context of your personal life, education, sports or business. In business you have to create new ideas every day, turn those ideas into action, go head-to-head with the competition and continue to serve your customers. Customers will accept mistakes, especially when you admit to them graciously. Customers demand *consistency*. You can't decide that today you're not going to be open for business; maybe you will re-open next week if the mood strikes you. Your customers will leave you and go to a competitor. You haven't shown them commitment. You haven't taken them seriously. Customers will decide that you don't deserve their business.

When you're on the road of commitment (yes, it is a road; it's long and winding), there is no such thing as "failure". Many business leaders believe that failure is one of the greatest learning opportunities. When something goes wrong, you learn something about your market and your customers that you hadn't appreciated before. That's not to say that mistakes aren't costly or aren't painful. They are. *The Tortoise and the Hare* is one of my favorite kids' stories as it teaches not only the disadvantage of boasting (i.e. everybody hates you), but more importantly it shows that if you stick to something long enough, you'll get there in the end, even beating the competition.

Commitment To An Organization Or Team Is A Worthwhile Pursuit

Although I don't encourage people to work long hours with no balance in their lives (we know this is a recipe for disaster), on a given day that might be exactly what's needed because you're committed to succeeding – succeeding for yourself, succeeding for the team, succeeding for the organization. Over the years, my time management skills have definitely been honed, but there have been occasions when a herculean effort was required to complete a project at work.

Teams Bond Through Adversity

One Friday I was thrown a rush job to pull together a quick analysis of the bank's market share for one of its financial products. The first thing I did was think about how to leverage the team, about what tasks needed to be performed and who could do those tasks best. I then gathered the team and explained the challenge. "Could everyone stay late?" I asked. They all bought in. By late afternoon the team had pulled together the nuts and bolts of the analysis. The data was all at our fingertips. The challenge was then to turn this information into a slick presentation, with conclusions, and ensure that all the numbers added up and made sense in the larger context of the market.

You can imagine how we were all lacking in energy at the end of yet another long work week. If our market share is X that means the total market share is Y. Do we have evidence that the total size of the market is in fact Y? The questions and double checking continued well past midnight. I remember midnight clearly. That was when the computers on the entire floor started shutting down, including of course the ones we were working on for the presentation. They were on some sort of energy-saving shut-down mode for the weekend. When this happened I really wondered whether we were going to pull it off.

We dialed our IT guy's cell number. He actually picked up at 12am! He coached us through the necessary procedures. Disaster averted; no meltdown. The taxi finally arrived at about 1am to take us home. We all had a great sense of accomplishment. I'm convinced that the guys who worked with me that night thought I had completely lost my mind. They could see I wasn't going to give up. What they don't know, perhaps, is that their commitment to finishing the job fuelled my inspiration. Although this was one of the most difficult deadlines, it was also one of the most rewarding experiences we had as a team.

Commitment Doesn't Guarantee Success

Does every commitment end in "success"? It most certainly doesn't. But that's when you've got to regroup, think about what you've learned and move on. When I was in my teens, life revolved around basketball. No, I mean *really* revolved around basketball. I was a fanatic. I practiced constantly, day in and day out. I was the captain of the team my sophomore year in high school. How could it be that with such a devotion to a sport and a team, I could then be cut from the squad in my junior year? This was *devastating* for me. My confidence was severely shaken. I just couldn't get my head around how this had happened. No basketball? What in the world was I going to do?

This turn of events led me to seek other avenues for fulfillment, which wouldn't have happened had I not been kicked off the team. It led me to seek opportunities to study abroad, opening up a whole new world. Am I saying that it was a good thing I didn't make the team? Even today, some thirty years later, I can feel the pain of being cut from the squad. I *loved* the game, but had to recognize that it wasn't meant to be and my life was heading in another direction. I can't say in my heart that

I'm *glad* it happened. Do I have regrets for being committed? No regrets. Being committed allowed me to be the best that I could be. I have just had to accept that my best wasn't good enough in that situation. Am I a better person for it? I'd have to say yes. It taught me about life.

Commitment Within The Family Unit

We've talked about commitment to combining career and family and about commitment to an organization. What does commitment within the family unit mean?

First and foremost, be committed to your partner. Always treat them with respect even when you're really angry. That's the irony, the ones you love the most are also the ones who can really get to you, make you angry. Some things are just not worth arguing over. None of us is perfect (especially me), so have some humility when you do get angry. Take a deep breath and give your partner some breathing room too. Do what you like to do to de-stress. My stress outlet is running. It really lifts my mood and changes my frame of mind and that way I avoid taking out my anger on someone else. Find your outlet and use it when called for. Avoid beating up the person who is your biggest supporter.

Being *committed to* your partner doesn't mean you feel madly in love with them every second – ok, maybe at the dating or newlywed stage, but human nature doesn't work that way. After the infatuation cools down you've got to deal with the realities. Whose turn is it to take out the trash? Who is going to change the baby's diapers? Do we have enough money to afford a mortgage? The longer you are together, the longer you will recognize and acknowledge your partner's annoying habits and weaknesses and more importantly, you will learn about your own shortcomings. I have found this to be one of the greatest benefits of being married. I've learned an awful lot about my own imperfections. This is why you need to have humility when living and working together as a team with your partner. Your partner is only human. You are only human.

INSTANT SATISFACTION IS NOT ACHIEVABLE

In our modern society it's hard not to want everything, right here, right now. I certainly forget sometimes that I've got to persevere through tough situations in order to enjoy the rewards at the end. Instant satisfaction is not achievable or realistic. I'm grateful for having been able to spend time with my husband's parents who were married for over fifty years. They showed me that even couples who are completely dedicated to one another have their moments.

Many weekends I'd see them argue about who did this or that. Dad had this habit of cleaning up after Mom. The problem was she hadn't finished what she was doing. She'd often get distracted by interesting conversations. She would leave the bread out on the counter to make a sandwich. Dad would then come in the kitchen and "helpfully" put the bread back into the cabinet to clean up. It was quite entertaining for spectators like me, but Mom, especially, would get really angry. One afternoon one of the kids suggested that Dad should put a sign outside on the lawn saying "I did it". That way they wouldn't have to spend time arguing. At this suggestion everyone in the room burst out laughing. Tension released. It was time to move on. Seeing an older couple deal with the normal friction of living together provides a useful illustration on how to approach a longer-term partnership. Don't sweat the small stuff.

You Are Your Kids' Biggest Advocate

The other significant commitment in the family unit is of course your commitment to your kids. You are their biggest advocate. You know them best and will stick by them through thick and thin. Keep at it – keep being a parent, providing guidance and advice, giving them opportunities to learn about the world through formal education, travel, social activities, sports or music. Often you will question yourself whether they are listening. Is this really worth it? They may pretend that they are not listening, but they are. It is sinking in.

When your kids are younger you may sometimes have to make decisions on their behalf because you feel that they don't have enough life experience for their opinion to override yours. Then as they mature they will be able to contribute to the decision-making process. Involve them. A good parent maintains a positive presence and influence throughout his or her child's life. This is why maternity or paternity leave isn't the end of the work-life balance issue, but rather just the beginning. Be committed to your kids by staying involved in their lives from early childhood through to the teenage years so that your relationship grows stronger. The relationship then will be strong enough to withstand the turbulent times. You won't regret the investment.

Be Committed To Your Kid's School

Your commitment to your children means you will be the number one person looking after their wellbeing and development. You will ensure that they are getting the right level of education and training based on their individual talents and personalities. Once you find the right school, be committed to it. As natural arbitrageurs kids are less likely to try to set you up against the school, the more they see you as the parent working collaboratively with the school.

At the beginning of each school year parents are sent reminders about different policies including the dress code. I've always felt that this was one way of demonstrating that I supported the school and was committed to following its rules and guidelines. I've had to refer to these policies more than once as my kids have challenged me on a number of occasions on what the rule book says about the length of boys' hair, the length of the girls' skirts, and the height of the girls' heels. The conversation goes something like, "Mom, *everyone* in the school has longer hair," or "Mom, *all* the girls in the school have higher heels than I do." I then reply, "That might be the case, but the school has sent out guidelines and it's my job to make sure my children follow those guidelines. I don't care about what other kids do. I only care about what *you* do."

Some Battles With The School
Will Be Worth Fighting

Despite this overall philosophy, I need to add a word of warning. Sometimes the school gets it wrong. We all make mistakes. You'll know when this happens and you'll need to pick your fights carefully to be effective. Otherwise, you'll get a reputation for complaining about everything. Some battles, however, will be worth the fight.

A number of years ago our older son was suspended from school for a week for "punching" another boy. It turned out that the two boys were horsing around rather than having a fight. The other boy was a friend, and continued to be a friend after the incident. My husband and I were furious as the punishment of suspension did not seem fit for the crime. A few years earlier when we learned that our son had been a victim of bullying for many months at the same school, the culprits were suspended. Were these incidences equal in seriousness? Taking a teenage boy out of school hurts the parents more than the child. How is he going to apply himself to serious work all day? We did go to battle (and lost), but we were able to ensure that our son was given some structured work to complete while he was out of school, which I doubt would have happened had we not made such a fuss. Our reaction also probably influenced the school's future policy on how it dealt with similar circumstances.

NO QUICK FIX - YOU'VE GOT TO BE IN IT FOR THE LONG HAUL

There Are Plenty of Reasons To Give Up

Despite the messages you might be hearing in the media, there is no quick fix. No special pill or fast diet is going to fix everything. Keeping it all together – the family, the work commitments, personal interests and your health – requires a long-term commitment. Every day you work at it, step by step. Some days will be easier than others. There will be lots of challenges in life. I've covered a few of these already. The point I'm making in this chapter is that unless you are *committed*, you are going to have more than enough excuses to say, "Forget it, it's too hard."

Aside from the whole issue of finding suitable childcare, what are some of the other significant challenges? Well, you may have elderly parents to look after, requiring you to contribute your time, finances or both. Your children may have issues at school: bullying, social issues, or a learning disability. You may have to deal with nasty politics in your work environment and wonder why you bother; is it worth the trade-off?

You will, however, reach your goal *if you stick with it.* Be tenacious! Don't accept the answers, "no you can't do that" or "no that's not possible". When things get tough, doubts do creep in. Don't give up. The difficult moments do pass. The political environment at work can change overnight. Don't let it de-rail you. Whatever problems your kids or parents are facing, there are plenty of resources to help sort things out, within the school, church, community as well as non-profit groups which support a variety of causes.

Being Committed Results In Incredibly Fulfilling Outcomes

When I was twenty four and newly married, my mother (who had been suffering from multiple sclerosis for nearly thirty years) was thrown out of her nursing home in New Jersey due to a lapse in insurance coverage. She had been in this nursing home for years. The insurer did a periodical review of her case and decided that they would not provide for custodial care (non-medical assistance), which was what the nursing home was deemed to be providing. When we learned of my mom's predicament, my husband didn't hesitate to announce in a matter of fact tone, "She's moving in with us." I was stunned. He recognized immediately that we were best placed to take care of her and he had no doubts that it was the right thing to do for my family. This was before having children. Taking care of a parent taught us many valuable and relevant lessons about how to balance work and family.

"Us two kids" had to function as a strong team in order to manage our respective jobs and organize nursing care. A huge financial burden was lifted off of our shoulders when the insurance company confirmed that they would cover the cost of qualified nursing care in our home. I'm not sure how we would have managed otherwise. We had been living in a small apartment on the third floor. One of the first steps we needed to take was to quickly find a house to rent which was all on one level in order to accommodate my mom's wheelchair. Once that was sorted I checked into which nursing agencies were available in the area and then set up a schedule for the nurses to come to our home Monday through Sunday. Despite her debilitating disease, my mother had an uplifting and positive presence. She didn't dwell on her situation or her pain. On the contrary, she was usually upbeat, smiling and so interested in *your* life and what *you* were doing. She also respected our privacy and didn't interfere in our personal business – an easy roommate to live with really.

Did we go through tough times? We sure did. We had to get up in the middle of night to turn my mom in her bed. (It pains me to remember how grumpy I sometimes was during those moments.) The doctors accused us of stealing her drugs (thanks a lot; this is what I get for helping out my own mother?). Her dosage had been steadily increasing in order to manage her pain and discomfort. Now comes the zinger. Mom expressed a wish not to have her life extended by extraneous means (DNR: Do Not Resuscitate). She had been through enough.

Even today, the thing I miss the most about having my mom with us is that it made all the trials and tribulations of daily life seem insignificant. So what, the car broke down again and we need to spend money on repairs. So what, the heating is malfunctioning and requires a complete overhaul. Like with children, caring for a parent gives you perspective and maturity which allows you to handle your professional commitments more wisely. Commitment isn't easy, it doesn't happen overnight, but being committed results in incredibly fulfilling outcomes. Keep a *long-term* view.

Be Committed To Progressing Your Career

Your career progression requires commitment. Think about it, plan for it, and take responsibility for it. It's too important to leave to chance or expect that someone else is going to look after you. Years ago people had life-time employment. Today it's almost non-existent. It's almost impossible to think that you might be working for the same organization for your entire life. This emphasizes the point that you cannot expect your employer to look after your career progression. Your current employer may certainly be motivated to keep you within the organization and therefore offer you training as well as opportunities to expand your skills. Employers, however, will not be able to connect the dots like you will be able to in order to help you get to where you want to be. Take control.

Investing In Your Career Pays Off

Furthering your career on top of raising a family and fulfilling your current responsibilities seems like more than a full plate, but investing in your career will pay off in the longer run. You'll have more gratification in your work. You'll be able to operate at a more advanced level. You are also likely to improve your financial situation. The additional financial resources can then be used to relieve some of the time pressures and domestic responsibilities. (The older you get, the more you have, and the more you have to take care of.). Where possible, take advantage of company training, night courses, higher degrees etc. Another option is to take a short-term break from employment, while you invest in further training and education, and then re-enter the workforce at a higher level.

Training and further education not only entail a time commitment, but also a financial commitment. Short-term pain, for longer-term gain. There's the cost of the training and education itself as well as perhaps the short-term loss of income if you do take a break. I only suggest taking a break from paid employment, if possible, to reduce the stress. If family finances are extremely tight, then that option may actually increase stress rather than decrease it. You'll need to find the right solution that works best for your situation.

Opportunities For Career Progression Coincide With Young Children

Unfortunately the opportunities for career progression often coincide with the most labor intensive phase of raising children, the earlier years. This phase is a pinch point, but it doesn't last forever. Keep the faith. Young children do grow up quickly and become more self sufficient. If you're happy with what you're doing and your children see that, then they will be happy. As I've said earlier, it's the strength and happiness of the family unit that affects the happiness of the children the most.

Your commitment to your career progression is like any other commitment; it's tough on a day-to day basis.

Although I absolutely love the life I lead, in the earlier years, particularly when the children still required a lot of physical care, I wondered how I could possibly keep it all together. I carefully considered the downside of opting out of career progression. You can feel stuck. Feeling stuck means that your level of responsibility in your job doesn't change and you start feeling less gratification in your work. You don't feel like you're reaching your true potential. You can do your current job brilliantly, but it's rather uneventful. When you're not feeling like you're being challenged at work, you start to doubt whether the tradeoff between work and family is worth it. Instead of feeling relieved that work's less demanding, you feel lethargic – that spark is gone.

The Impact Of Your Career Progression On Kids' Schooling

Once you have kids and they've reached school age, you focus a lot on education. Which school? How far is the school from work? How far is it from after school care? This major decision may be hijacked if you or your partner has the opportunity for a new job in a new location. Without a doubt it's very disruptive for a child to change schools. And when they reach an age when they start taking standardized tests, which will determine their next stage of education, your life tends to take shape around these exams.

A number of American families we have met since we moved to the UK have decided exactly when they will return to the US so that their kids can enter back into the US school system at the "right" time. What's the "right" time? What is the "right" decision? There's no one answer, or right answer. When you are faced with a decision to move, you and your partner will need to take all viewpoints into consideration and decide which scenario works best for the family. It's likely that one of your careers will be impacted. The world's not perfect. There will be pros and cons to every decision. As long as whatever you decide you decide as a team, things will work out.

When we considered moving back to the UK when our kids were three and six, we thought it would be easy for them to adjust, it would be the "right" time. Our daughter had just turned six and was just about to start primary school. Little did we know that in the UK they start formal primary education at the age of five. This meant that our daughter joined a class in which every student had already been reading for a year. In addition to that, she was in a school that wasn't very international. She felt intimidated. She felt like she stood out. The situation did unsettle her and she did struggle for a number of months. It was agonizing to watch. I felt horrible. What had I done? I began to question whether we had made the right decision to move on account of my career. Kids are incredibly resilient and do bounce back quickly, however. Thank goodness (for my sake) for that. She did get through it, made friends, eventually settled into the new school and became a very proficient reader at that.

Give And Take – Keep The Partnership Alive

In a dual-career family there will be a lot of give and take regarding opportunities for career progression. Within today's global economy, location could be anywhere. There will be opportunities in other cities, other states, and other countries. Different opportunities will require different travel commitments and working hours. You and your partner will need to discuss the possible scenarios and accept that the stars might not be perfectly aligned on all fronts when you make your final decision on a career path. The important thing is the give and take, and keeping the partnership alive.

CHAPTER EIGHT

Follow the 3 C's:
The Second C is Communication

BE CLEAR ABOUT WHAT YOU
MEAN AND MEAN WHAT YOU SAY

COMMUNICATION IS THE SECOND C. Be clear about what you mean, mean what you say, and then finally *do* what you say (in other words practice what you preach). Communication can be tricky. We all have had different experiences and reference points and therefore the exact same message can be interpreted completely differently by different individuals.

Clear & Consistent Communication Creates Trust

In business you lose all authority once you are wishy washy or don't mean what you say, regardless of your job title or position. In the workplace, unlike at home, your peers and colleagues are unlikely to tell you that you're full of it (although that's what they may be thinking). You say one thing, but they know you do something else. You are inconsistent and your word can't be relied upon. Organizations with clear consistent messages, backed up by consistent behavior, are likely to be more successful. Their customers trust them. They trust their product and services. They trust that the organization will respond when they are unhappy or unsatisfied in any way. This is how an organization builds brand recognition.

Following the discovery of a fault in their strollers, Maclaren suffered a huge PR disaster due to their inconsistent messaging and treatment of customers. Yes, their strollers were faulty, but they committed a worse crime. They treated their US customers differently than their UK customers. In the US there was a complete recall of all of the strollers, which it was claimed had slivered children's fingers when closing. In the UK, on the other hand, there was no recall. Instead, the UK clients were offered kits to repair the strollers. Maclaren failed to recognize the power that individual customers now have readily at their disposal - it's called the internet. While the company could control traditional channels of communication, it could not prevent customers going online and sharing their experiences. Trust in the organization was damaged because global customers received less than consistent and respectful treatment. As you can imagine, once this discrepancy became public, the company changed its policy and all customers were treated equally.

Kids Call You Out On Any Inconsistencies!

Unlike the professional world, kids will call you out as soon as they spot an inconsistency – which they will do sooner or later as they are very adept at this type of analysis. Children are building a database in their own heads about what's right and what's wrong. When you say one thing and do another, it creates a short circuit. "You said this, but you're doing that? This does not compute." Communication is only as good as the actions that follow.

If you tell your kids smoking is very bad for you, but then you smoke, guess what they will do? The danger is one inconsistent message can damage your credibility in all areas. You tell your kids to respect their elders, their parents, yet maybe they don't see you caring for their grandparents, your parents. With kids it's like they have an internal video recorder and everything you say and do can be replayed in their head at any given moment. Perhaps one of the reasons kids can remember the past so clearly is that they have less to remember. I'm often astounded by the level of detail that my children from toddler to teenage years can recall about an event which I had long forgotten, especially if it involved me making a "mistake".

Follow-Through Is One Of The Basics Of Good Parenting

When your children are toddlers is when you've really got to nail this skill! It's the basics of parenting. If you don't communicate clearly with your toddler and your actions are not consistent with your words, you're in deep trouble. You are setting the benchmark which your kids will refer to in future interactions. They quickly learn which adults will follow through on their words and which ones won't. One of the worst things you can do as parent is to lay down an ultimatum and then not follow through.

The *Supernanny* TV program demonstrates the possible outcomes from various approaches to communication and subsequent actions. It's not easy as it sounds. You'll have the tendency to shout out all kinds of threats and consequences in the heat and frustration of the moment. Only shout out the ones that you can then implement. It's tough to follow through when they look at you with such sweet, innocent faces. Don't fall for it. You've got to follow through. Otherwise you will live in false hope that they are going to be better behaved now that you've threatened them (even though you didn't follow through with the stated consequence). It won't happen. On the other hand, if you *do* follow through, and you do this *consistently*, you'll have control over your kids. Your job as a parent becomes easier once you've established a pattern of credibility – your kids will know that you mean what you say. Also be sure to agree with your partner what standard of behavior is acceptable and which type of threats should be used. Even toddlers can spot an arbitrage and will go to the parent who is going to cave in to their demands. Kids are cleverly-wired human beings.

TO NAVIGATE THROUGH CHANGE YOU NEED STRONG COMMUNICATION SKILLS

Keep Balance At Home By Communicating With Your Home Team

At home how can you possibly get the balance right if you're not communicating with your team members about what's going on? The lifestyle you lead is fast paced and if things are to be in balance, it's essential that you are constantly communicating with the key stakeholders: partner, children, childcare provider and the school.

Keeping in sync with your partner will at times feel challenging. There will be many aspects of your life to coordinate with them, from work and travel commitments to kids' school events and activities; the social calendar, home repairs, and wider family issues (eg elderly parents). Can you make the next parents' consultation evening? Have you contacted the lawyer about updating our wills? Did the quote come in yet for the roof repairs? Short, but frequent communication tends to be more effective than longer conversations.

Use Technology To Manage Family As Well As Work Logistics

Before the internet and cell phones, I used to leave my husband any important messages on his voicemail, which was considered advanced technology at the time. (Yes, I am really that old.) I knew that when he picked up a message he'd be in a work frame of mind. The message would be taken on board and noted. Nowadays, email, cell phones, blackberries and Iphones do make communication much easier, even though it's harder to escape from work.

As a couple, my other half and I have found that communicating by email is incredibly efficient. Sometimes it gets so busy that you forget whether you actually told your partner about an upcoming event. Referring back to sent emails you're reassured that you actually did send a message and you haven't completely lost your mind. Our email messages are generally short and to the point, highlighting any particular dates or times that need to be noted. Take advantage of technology when you can to help with the logistics of managing family as well as managing work.

Stay On Top Of Information From The School

You'll need to pay close attention to what's happening with your child at school and at home, as you will not always be there if you're combining career and family. That means you will need to be diligent about reading any notes that the school sends home. What information about the school day has been relayed by your child, by the babysitter? The point is to stay on top of these messages so that you can respond quickly while the situation is still easy to manage.

Be Open To Receiving Feedback From Your Childcare Provider

Your childcare provider will obviously play a pivotal role in observing your child's behavior. Be open to listening to her feedback and share any observations you've had. Perhaps you've noticed that your child's handwriting doesn't seem to be developing as well as it should. What view does your childcare provider have on this? Has the school mentioned anything? Having this type of discussion will allow you to determine whether the matter is serious enough to require further action. Should the school be advised; could it be dyslexia? When an issue does arise, discuss and agree the proposed action plan with your childcare provider (and with your partner of course).

Through this type of short, but frequent dialogue, you will be able to manage your child's development. Your child is growing and changing constantly, so you need to remain flexible and open to receiving feedback on progress both positive and negative. Try not to take it too personally when it's negative. Just deal with it.

BUSINESSES NEED TO ADAPT TO A CHANGING ENVIRONMENT

The external environment doesn't stand still either. In this age of electronic communication and a global economy, it's more the case today than ever before. Businesses are faced with an external environment which is a moving target. The market niche you have today could easily be gone tomorrow, unless you stay on top of innovation, customers' preferences, and major trends. The needs of your employees are also changing. Young employees today are motivated as much by lifestyle options as they are by money. Your workforce may be aging. Your employees' personal situations may be shifting, and their requirements for healthcare cover or working hours may be changing in response.

To deal with the shifts in the marketplace, a business will need to solicit constant feedback from its clients, employees, and suppliers. It needs to communicate its strategy. A business, like any effective team, needs everyone pulling in the same direction. Without a clearly articulated plan with some simple and clear action steps, it will be tough to successfully capture new market opportunities.

In this recent recession many businesses have been struggling. That's when it's more important than ever to tell it like it is – people aren't stupid and don't buy the cleverly worded euphemism for bad news. I have seen corporate communication departments work feverishly at coming up with clever words to lessen the blow of mistakes, poor results, only to find that employees feel insulted for being treated like children. Honesty is the key to building trust. When trust is at the heart of communication, messages are more readily received and understood. The same principle applies to communication at home.

Set Clear And High Expectations

In a fast moving environment it's also critical that you are clear about what you expect from others, at home and at work. You will also want to give others space so they can do things their way, but at the same time you've got to be really clear about what you expect. Doing everything yourself is just as ineffectual at home as it is at work. At work they call it micromanaging and it's one of the factors that can result in stress (for the person doing the micromanaging as well as the person who is being micromanaged). As an employee, you're also stressed when your boss isn't clear about what he or she expects. In some ways the unknown is worse than having difficult targets to meet.

I am known for being direct and saying it like it is. The upside is that everyone around me, regardless of the environment, knows what I expect, and they know what they can expect from me. If you're committed to caring for my children and then you book an impromptu vacation without discussing it first, I'll tell you that you have acted irresponsibly and that I expect more. This is not a one-way street. I would also act irresponsibly if I didn't give *you* any notice of my vacation plans. What's amazing though is that when you set high standards for others and yourself, the overall level of achievement is higher than it would have been had you set low standards. Everyone likes a goal when presented in the right way. Be clear about the level of quality and effort you expect, and give others room to shine.

OPEN-DOOR POLICY WORKS AT HOME TOO

It's the little steps that count – little, but frequent. Check in with your childcare provider every day - it just takes a minute. Ask her how she's feeling. The parent-childcare provider relationship is no different from any of your professional relationships in that way. The big difference is it *is* personal – it's about *your* child. A childcare provider has her own personal needs, goals and ambitions and the more you understand these, the stronger your relationships will be.

Encourage the childcare provider to discuss things with you. Like at work, have an open-door policy. Dealing with issues as they crop up is so much easier than letting them fester. By doing this you are also showing respect for the valuable job the childcare provider performs. I tend to be very task-oriented and therefore have to remind myself at home and at work that tasks are completed by *people* and you've got to take a minute to check in on their health and wellbeing. Are they happy? What's on their mind? I've been surprised how much you can learn by just listening.

Recognize When People Are Not Opening Up

Years ago I had a nanny who had a unique talent for holding back on her concerns. It used to drive me mad. She would raise issues sometimes weeks or months after the event. I wish I had recognized this tendency earlier so I could have managed it better. I should have done a better job in getting her to open up, using some of those nifty management skills I had learned at work.

One evening when I came home from work the nanny seemed slightly agitated. I asked her if everything was ok. She replied, "The wages you left me four months ago were not enough, it was short by £20." "Four months ago!" I spurted out in utter frustration. "Why didn't you tell me as soon as you realized the mistake?" It seemed as though she had been mulling this over for months. It was eating away at her. She became angrier and angrier. I wasn't angry at all that she brought it up. I try to get through the household admin stuff very quickly during the weekend and sometimes I do make mistakes. (Haste makes waste?) What made me angry was that she didn't have the maturity to address her concern with me straight away. Because she let it fester, a mountain was made out of a mole hill.

Establish Ground Rules: No Passing The Buck

Frequent, open and brief communication is the way to go. There is one word of caution, however, with the open-door policy. You might be bombarded with "problems" unless you also set some ground rules. One ground rule is that anyone who raises a problem should be prepared to offer a few options or solutions as well. Otherwise, the "monkey" jumps from the person who had a concern onto your back. Before you know it, you won't be able to withstand the weight of all the monkeys on your back. Within the team dynamic everyone still has to feel responsible for solving the challenge at hand. They don't have the option of just passing the problem onto someone else.

Like most kids, our kids complain. They moan, "You didn't choose the right movie. You didn't book the right holiday. I don't like the food you cooked." Firstly, we reply, "Don't forget about all the kids in the world who have much less than you do." Secondly, we reply, "You can take the initiative the next time to sort it out yourselves." This doesn't stop the complaining altogether, but it does reduce it. Kids also learn that they won't get away with just passing the buck to someone else. We're all in this together.

Avoid Boiling Point With Your Partner

Back when my husband and I were married there was a requirement to attend a pre-marriage retreat if you wanted to get married in the Church. I know it sounds really old fashioned. We thought the same. It was a weekend event and we had to do a lot of role playing and break out into discussion groups. Despite our skepticism we came away quite surprised by the results. The advice we were given has stood the test of time.

Tip number one: Never go to bed angry. This practice forces you to address whatever it is that's bugging you. Also, don't take for granted that you will have tomorrow. You may not have tomorrow to say you're sorry if that's what's needed. Live each day to its fullest.

Tip number two: Don't go for the jugular. No matter how angry you get, don't say things in the heat of the moment that you will regret later. Although you want to deal with issues as they come up, you don't want to have it out each time, escalating the conflict and making it into a bigger deal than it needs to be.

Deliver The Right Message In The Right Place At The Right Time

Pick the right times to discuss the right topic. You'll learn this through trial and error. I have found that the worst time for discussing anything important in our household is just before dinner. We are all pretty high energy people, and without a full stomach the situation always seems darker and more complicated than it really is. Avoiding moments when you're feeling really tired is also a useful tip. Ever notice how much brighter the world seems once you've had a good night's rest?

Effective communication means choosing the right place and the right time as well as delivering the right message. Creating the right place can also mean creating the atmosphere to encourage someone else to open up and communicate. (Why didn't someone tell me this earlier? I could have avoided many unpleasant moments.) It's not just about you delivering your message. In the workplace it might be too hectic or stressful to allow individuals to feel relaxed enough to have a frank conversation. It also may be on a subject that requires more than a few minutes. Be sensitive to these situations and suggest alternative settings. Perhaps get together for a coffee or maybe meet up for a glass of wine after work.

Establish Common Ground With Your Children

The same concept applies with children. If you really need to understand what an individual child is thinking or feeling, create a special time for him or her, especially if you have more than one child. Children behave differently in a group. On their own they are given more of an opportunity to express their individuality. You want to create a situation which makes them feel comfortable and relaxed so they can reveal their inner thoughts. If you ask a child, "How was school?" The most common reply is "Fine". Yup, that's it. They are at times not very communicative. Try open-ended questions: "What was your favorite part of today? Tell me what happened."

Establishing common ground with younger children is far easier and more straightforward than finding commonality with teenagers. Younger children tend to be involved in many extracurricular activities which welcome and sometimes even require parent participation. I recall the coach of my daughter's gym club encouraging the parents to set up the gym floor and equipment before each practice session. This gave us an opportunity to get to know the other girls and their parents as well as all of the coaches. Getting to know your children's friends is also a great way to learn about your own kids. Their friends are a reflection of them. This could be a good sign or a bad sign. Keep your eyes peeled. The drive to and from the club also gave us an opportunity to just talk. By creating opportunities for your kids to tell you what's on their mind, you can provide small doses of guidance along the way.

Older children, especially teenagers, on the other hand are struggling to be distinct and separate from you. Communication is much more of challenge. They are establishing their independence. Before our daughter decided which university she wanted to go to, my husband arranged a lunch with her and a few of his female colleagues. His hope was that his colleagues would provide our daughter with advice and counsel on how to go about choosing the right university for her area of concentration, which was medicine. This was a real olive branch. It showed our daughter that he did recognize she was no longer a child. Although this situation didn't necessarily create dedicated air time just for her, the focus was mostly on her and it created new common ground on which father and daughter could relate. During this lunch our daughter shared her thoughts about university in a mature manner which would have been difficult to achieve at home, especially with two younger brothers competing for attention.

CHAPTER NINE

Follow The 3 Cs: The Third C Is Conflict Management

CONFLICT IS A NATURAL PART OF YOUR PERSONAL AND PROFESSIONAL LIFE

CONFLICT MANAGEMENT IS THE THIRD C. I always get a strange look when I tell people that conflict management was the most valuable skill I learned in business school. It wasn't the net present value calculations or statistics course that I found most valuable in business, but rather the ability to handle and embrace conflict. I mean it: *embrace* conflict. When you work in a large group, you're bound to come up against conflict almost every hour of every single day. That's because we are human. It's part of what defines us. The first step in dealing with conflict is to accept that it's not a bad situation, but rather a natural part of life – family life as well as professional life. Thinking of it in this way won't get rid of the conflict, but it allows you not to take it personally.

When you accept that conflict is a natural state of being human, you are able to deal with conflict in a *positive* way. Just because you are disagreeing with someone, doesn't mean you are behaving badly. It can often mean you're doing precisely what you should be doing. You're raising questions that need to be taken into consideration in order for the group to make a sound decision. Being part of a team by definition means there's conflict. Each one of us is unique. Each team member has a distinct personality, talent and skill set.

Romantic Partnerships Have Built-In Conflict

In romantic relationships the partner you chose is likely to have an opposite personality to yours – opposite, yet complementary. Opposites attract as we saw earlier. This means that your partnership has built-in conflict; you're one personality type, they are the other. Even though your differing personalities are complementary, you may not always relish those differences. The differences will at times mean that you get on each other's nerves. Why can't she be more patient, like me? Why can't he be more direct, like me? Being like you isn't the answer. If he were like you, you wouldn't be attracted to him and you wouldn't make a compatible team.

Families Have Built-In Conflict

It sounds strange to say that a family, the one facet of life dedicated to nurturing and caring for us as individuals, has built-in conflict, but it's true. Anyone who has siblings, especially lots of them, can tell you all about conflict. If you're a child and there's more than one of you in a family, the battle to capture your parents' attention begins at a very young age. Sibling rivalry is a harsh reality, but good training for the outside world which you eventually are going to have to venture into. In the outside world you're competing with everyone for attention: the guy you're interested in getting to know better, the teacher who you're trying to get to help you or the boss you're trying to get to recognize your talents. You should thank your brother or sister for preparing you for the real world and forget about all those bumps, bruises (bites?) and hurt feelings.

You will also be competing for material things in a sibling relationship. How come she got two scoops of ice cream and I only got one scoop? She got a new bike for Christmas. How come I didn't get a new bike? My younger sister and I are less than two years apart so these types of conversations were plentiful in our house growing up. My mother used to diffuse our arguments by saying that each of us gets what we need, not what we want. Her wise remarks made us feel guilty. She reminded us that we were in fact each unique. It did make the pain easier to bear, although it didn't relieve it completely. My husband, one of eight children, reminds our kids that they should be thankful for the abundance of healthy, good food we enjoy at home. He tells stories of fighting for "crumbs" at every meal. He was always mindful that any meal had to be split into ten equal portions. Two slices of ham was out of the question. One was the accepted norm, between two slides of thin, plain, white bread.

Fighting For Time & Attention Is Common For Busy Families

Conflict within our immediate family has mostly been centered on getting attention, even though we're not a particularly large family. With busy lifestyles finding time and attention for each family member is always a struggle. When all of our children were living at home and we had a full-time nanny, I would witness this fight for attention between the kids, and even between the kids and nanny when I would come home from work.

As I walked through the door, each of the kids would start vying for space and attention, followed by bargaining. I was certain that these negotiation skills would serve them well later in life. Each of them pleaded their case, "Mom, can I download a computer game? Mom, can I go to Charlie's after school on Friday? Mom, can we buy new baking sheets to make cookies?" These were all decisions that the nanny wanted me to comment on before she took action. I have to say it was nice to feel wanted, missed and respected as one of the key decision makers. I thought, "How boring it would be to come home to an empty house!" This was entertainment at its best.

146

Professional Teams Have Built-In Conflict

Strong teams are formed by including individuals who have varied backgrounds, personalities, and perspectives. These differences actually help the team dynamics and make the team stronger. It follows that strong teams will also have built-in conflict. Although as a professional I may gravitate towards colleagues who look and behave like me, it's better to chose team members who are different than I am.

I learned first-hand how a group made up of different personality types can be advantageous thanks to a clever exercise devised by one of my marketing professors. The professor divided the class up into groups, putting like personalities in the same group (without us knowing). We had all taken personality tests so *he* knew our personality profiles. We learned that we were each a mix of four types, with one type being dominant. The four types were: Director (quick to make decisions, likes to be in position of power and control); Socializer (extravert, likes to talk to people); Relater (sensitive to the needs of others); and Critical Thinker (detailed oriented, more introverted).

The task of each group was to agree on the type of company they were going to set up, its mission statement and key competitive advantage. The exercise was a complete disaster (intentionally so). I was surrounded by director types just like me. No problem being with similar personality types, but when you are working together on a group project, it can generate a lot of tension.

I remember the first meeting where everyone turned up, and just like me, had too many balls in the air, very crunched for time and impatient. We were bouncing off the walls. Each of us was ready to make a decision about the company, but that was problem. We each had our own view and were quite assertive in pushing that view forward. There were no Relater personalities to help us work through the differences. We needed other personality types to help move the discussion forward. Conflict is good when it's productive. This wasn't productive.

After a few group meetings where the other groups were experiencing similar frustrations, our professor told us that we had been set up to fail. In the Relater group no one could make a decision about anything. They were all concerned about how the others might feel. The Socializers barely had time to talk about the company assignment as they spent a lot of time chatting about which area of the country they came from, where they worked etc. When they did finally start talking about the company, they were talking over one another. The Critical Thinker group got bogged down in the detail, making little progress towards a formation of a company. That exercise really did drive the point home for me. I actually lived through the concept instead of reading it in a book.

From a business perspective you can clearly see from this exercise the benefit of having diversity within a team. In addition to reaching more well-rounded decisions, it also helps the team function better. At the same time you are building a team of varied personalities, skill sets and experience, you are also building a team that by definition will gel together better. Within an organization you also have various functions or specializations that need to be performed. Each of these functions lends itself to a certain personality type. You want the Directors and Socializers to be in charge of external communications. You want the Critical Thinkers in charge of quality control, and you want the Relaters to head up the human resource department.

Conflict Is An Effective Risk Management Tool

Conflict used in the right way acts like a risk management mechanism. If one team member has a proposal, the built-in conflict of the group allows the other members to kick the tires. What are the pros and cons of the proposal? If all the members were similar, you would come to similar conclusions and miss an aspect of the situation which could be quite dangerous. This is the risk of group think. You get comfortable because of the numbers: everyone agrees that your decision is the right one. Group think is to be avoided. Before understanding team dynamics I truly believed that I could get things done quicker on my own. In my youth I also interpreted feedback as criticism and took offence when others didn't perfectly agree with what I had done or proposed. I interpreted feedback as a reflection of others being pessimists or glass half-empty kind of people, rather than ideas for improving upon my original proposal.

I realized through practice – being forced to work in groups – that it's not humanly possible to consider all the angles of a situation, and that the quality of the end product is always better when you incorporate feedback. I also matured and saw that others were not always being negative and were in fact providing constructive ideas. The complexity today in almost every field is mind boggling. It demands talent from many disciplines. Of course you do have to balance building consensus with delaying implementation or getting the job done, i.e. the consultation period can't go on indefinitely. At some point you've got to hit the button and go. If you've involved others, however, you'll know that the chances of success have increased substantially.

Businesses By Design Have Competing Departments

Businesses and other professional organizations have checks and balances in place to keep people honest, maintain standards of quality control, and review key decisions. Organizations will have on the face of it *competing* departments or divisions. The structure of a trading floor is a good example. Traders are pitted against sales people and vice versa. Traders look after the risk profile of their trading positions, while sales people represent their clients' interest. Sometimes these interests are matched and a good trade happens. Often times, however, a trader will complain that the sales person's motive is solely to earn a commission. Sales people complain that traders say they want to build a customer business, but they won't trade with a customer unless it perfectly suits their portfolio.

The conflict doesn't end at the sales-trader relationship. There are many other departments who oversee or control the activities on a trading floor. Product control, for example, cross checks the traders' profit calculations and raises concerns when the profit or loss can't be explained by market movements. The compliance department runs periodic checks to determine whether sales people and traders are following regulatory guidelines. Power technically is not wielded by one group to the detriment of risk management. (Where did we go wrong in the recent financial crisis? Hint: group think.)

Governmental Organizations Have Checks & Balances

The US Government is also a good example of the checks and balances within an organization. The government includes three independent branches: the Executive Branch (the President), the Legislative Branch (Congress) and the Judicial Branch (the legal system/Supreme Court). There is constant conflict and tension between these branches of government. Too much power in one set of hands is dangerous.

As a US citizen, I take great comfort in this built-in conflict. It allows for sensible debate to occur before major changes are made permanent. Healthcare reform raised questions about whether it was constitutional to require individual citizens to buy health insurance – a question for the judicial branch which is still pending. Many of the social programs instigated by Franklin D

Roosevelt during the Depression were later overturned as being unconstitutional. Checks and balances are like a security system. They protect organizations from making decisions based on a single interest group or view.

Deal With Conflict Head-On

Don't shy away from conflict. Capitalize on it to make your business better. Use it to strengthen your personal relationships. The adrenaline that gets activated when you're under pressure can be a great motivator to take action. You feel compelled not to accept the status quo; something's gotta give. The adrenaline, if not controlled, can backfire on you and worsen the situation. You need to harness it and use it to get everyone motivated to move things forward. Before deciding to take action as a result of a conflict, take a minute to reflect on how important the conflict is. Do a quick cost/benefit analysis in your head. Is it worth taking action or is it really not that important an issue and therefore I should let it ride? It's the important conflicts that you want to take head on. The others may not be worth the effort.

Some Conflicts Are Worth The Effort

One New Year 's Eve the family had planned on going to the health club for a work-out, swim and sauna before the club closed for the New Year. We pretty much scheduled our whole day around getting to the club by 3pm in order to be out by the 4pm close. When we arrived at 3.01pm and swiped our cards at the barrier, just behind two other members, we were stopped by one of the trainers. He announced, "Last entry was at 3pm." "Not a problem," we replied, "We'll be out by four." The trainer explained further that the club had a sign posted all week that last entry was at 3pm and that they had to make the cut-off somewhere. "3.01 is not the appropriate cut off," we demanded, "Especially given that you have our word that we will be out by 4pm. Surely that's your objective."

The trainer wouldn't budge. We asked to speak to the manager. We were left waiting in the small entrance hall for twenty minutes before the manager finally came out to meet us. By that time we were extremely agitated, feeling like animals penned up in a cage. As members of the club for over seventeen years, and having never been late in paying the membership fees, we found this treatment insulting beyond belief. The manager apologized, but said he could not let us in. His staff had simply followed procedure. Our posture then became extremely aggressive (still verbal, no punches). Was this any way to be spending New Year's Eve?

I thought to myself, "Is this level of aggression and conflict really necessary?" I decided that it was because the club was either going to have to be more customer-oriented or I'd take my pocketbook somewhere else. The manager was firm in his decision, but he did try to reassure us that he would personally investigate the situation and come back to us (too little, too late in our minds). Later that afternoon to our surprise the manager did call us at home. He apologized profusely for the club's behavior. His verbal apologies were followed up in writing. He even sent us flowers.

Why was this worth the fight? This very negative experience resulted in two positive outcomes: firstly, we found a new club with the added benefit of tennis facilities as well as more expansive childcare; secondly, our old club has taken on board our feedback and is improving its business model. The club still lost out on our business as even their improved model can't compete with the tennis facilities and extensive children's activities at our new club.

The Power Of Facing Conflict

Working in a male-dominated industry for years, I found that by not shying away from conflict – having the guts to discuss an awkward issue with just about anybody – I quickly gained respect from peers, subordinates and bosses. As the business manager of a trading floor, I had to monitor performance of the various business units, and then meet up with each of the business heads on a monthly basis to discuss their results. I wasn't exactly Miss Popular. I felt like Big Brother sometimes. But Tom Peters, the management guru, was right: what gets measured gets done. These could have been awkward moments, especially if a business wasn't performing, but I always kept it professional and respectful. (And I did respect them. Running a business is no small feat.)

Don't Make It Personal

It's when others don't treat us with respect that we get mad. This is one of the reasons why conflict can escalate. We don't get as angry at someone who disagrees with us as we do at someone who treats us like our opinions are stupid or invalid. If this happens you simply say, "Your comments make me *feel* like my opinion doesn't matter." You can never argue with what someone else is *feeling*. Only they know what they are feeling. Don't make it personal. It's ok to criticize the opinion, but not the person.

Key phrases to use to move a heated discussion into more amicable territory include, "I understand your position. I can see where you're coming from. And I can see why you would say that." This sort of language is very comforting to the person who's upset as long as it's genuine. When giving your opinion or views, it's useful to start with the phrase, "In my opinion/ view, I think it may..." That way you don't sound arrogant and give the appearance that you know it all. As with all of my advice these strategies work across a range of settings. Try it out. I'm sure you won't have to wait too long for a tense situation to arise.

CHAPTER TEN

The Magic Of Problem Solving

"DOES PROBLEM SOLVING DESERVE ITS OWN CHAPTER?" I wondered. It is in fact mentioned in almost every chapter. But then I thought, "That's the point. Problem solving helps us to apply the values, strategies and skills needed to deal with daily life. It's the ultimate facilitator and it works like magic." Without problem solving you'd be hard pressed to be able to make career *and* family work.

Another way of looking at "problems" is that they are unexpected outcomes. We weren't, for instance, expecting that someone would react in a certain way, or that a certain technical or logistical issue would arise. That's why we refer to it as a "problem". We don't have ready-made solutions. Think about how utterly dull our lives would be if we knew what was going to happen, and exactly how we would deal with each eventuality. Life would be completely predictable. How mind-numbing would that be?

CREATING NEW REALITIES THROUGH PROBLEM SOLVING

Problem solving demands a certain outlook or propensity to move forward. There's no time to get stuck into a no-can-do attitude. If you think you can't do, you won't do it. That's the first step. The second step is then brainstorming and involving others to generate new ideas and test the feasibility of those ideas. It's through your ability to solve problems that you are able to handle many aspects of your life. You're in the driver's seat. You're in control of your destiny.

Problems Provide Focus For A Team

A "problem" provides teams with an opportunity to focus on a common goal. Problem solving seen in this light is an opportunity to be seized, rather than something to agonize over. Don't shy away. Take the bull by the horns and make something extraordinary out of the situation. It's often in moments of urgency, deadlines, panic and stress, that a team can really get their juices churning and perform well. It's very similar to a sporting competition. The adrenaline generated by the difficulty of the event provides the team with the necessary energy boost to excel.

When you're solving problems you have to operate in the two dimensions as I mentioned on the chapter about teams: task orientation and people orientation. Task orientation requires you to think about the logistics and technical points of the matter. The people orientation is where the "soft" skills are required. Don't be confused by the word *soft*. These soft skills are equally important in solving problems as a team (although I never believed it when I was in my early twenties). Remember to take a minute and really empathize with the other party. Listen to their suggestions and views. Understand what concerns them the most, and above all, respond to their comments with respect.

Communicating About Problems Is Part of Daily Life

Problems are just another name for challenges, concerns, worries, issues, difficulties, troubles, so it's pretty far reaching. By discussing concerns you can start to sort through which ones deserve more focus. Talking it through helps clarify things in your own mind. By communicating you're also getting it off your chest. You feel better just by talking about it. By virtue of others listening, your spirits our lifted and you start feeling more positive about being able to figure out an answer. You're better equipped to come up with an answer now that your mindset is focused on the positive.

Others See Things You Can't See

Sharing your thoughts with others leads you to new pathways that you hadn't even considered before. Often others can see solutions you can't see because you're too close to the detail and the emotion. I'm sure you've had the experience where something was really bothering you and you discussed it with a friend. Then your friend proposed a simple, but incredibly effective solution. It was staring you in the face, but you couldn't see it. And you felt silly because the concern really wasn't that troublesome to begin with.

Don't Send An Email When You're Angry

It's worth emphasizing that you should never send an email to communicate about a concern where there is a lot of emotion involved. As we said earlier, communication can be tricky and when we humans are in an emotional state, communication is more likely to go awry. If you have no choice but to communicate by email (or other written communication), then do several drafts before sending. Take a break in between drafts. Once you send it, there's no taking it back.

In my early twenties I worked in an accounting function for a small consulting firm. An older woman was in charge of payroll and she was considered to be a real veteran. She had been with the company since its founding some twenty years earlier. I was really angry about her lack of follow-up on a particular topic. In the heat of the moment I put something in writing and sent it to one of the consultants. Luckily for me, most of the consultants working for the company were interested in developing people. Having received my memo, this consultant took me aside and pulled out my note, which in the light of day looked very unprofessional. I wanted to crawl under the desk. He explained in a fatherly manner why my approach was not recommended. My ego was dented, but I learned a valuable lesson.

A Good Time Manager Solves The Problem Of The 24-Hour Clock

In order to be organized you need to be able to manage your time effectively. You make time for the important things, the priorities. Finding time requires being *creative*. How do I shift my schedule around so that I can make room for the things I should be focusing on? By being an effective time manager you are solving the problem of there simply being only twenty four hours in a day.

Businesses have been created around this need to free up time. Career and family exacerbates the problem of the limited clock; you've got even more things to fit into a short space of time. This means that families need help in all kinds of areas – food shopping, clothes shopping, organizing parties, house-cleaning and garden maintenance. The growth of internet shopping demonstrates how many families value services which save them time.

Concierge services and party organizers (including children's parties) would have been unheard in my parents' day. Such time-saving services allow families to spend time on sport and other activities during the weekend. Take advantage of these time-saving goods and services and use the time saved to *enjoy* your weekends. In this way you're beating the twenty four hour clock. You've been able to figure out how to take care of life's necessities, while also finding time to exercise, have fun and relax.

PROBLEMS, LIKE CONFLICT, ARE A NATURAL PART OF LIFE

Similar to accepting that conflict is a natural part of life, you need to accept that problems are also a natural part of life. Without problems most of us wouldn't have jobs. Accepting this fact allows you to calm down... nothing's wrong in your life. You're just living it and that's why you're faced with challenges.

When I was in high school I ran cross country races. During one of those races through a heavily wooded area I caught poison ivy – it covered my face. It was disgusting. I felt like a leper. I refused to go to school with my severely disfigured face and at fourteen you know how important looks and fashion are. I remember my dad trying to comfort me. He responded to my distress by saying, "Chrissy, if you never do anything in life you won't get hurt. That wouldn't be very interesting, would it? You've caught this rash because you were actually *doing* something. That's a wonderful accomplishment." Those words left a big impression on me. Our bumps and bruises show that we were *in* the fight, which is the most important thing. Standing on the sidelines of life would be a dreary existence.

You Can Change Things – You Can Make A Difference

It's up to you how you respond to tough situations. You can let them defeat you, or let them make you a better person. My older son worked on the Heathrow Airport renewal project this past summer. What a fantastic opportunity. He learned as much about people as he did about engineering. One Sunday afternoon he was helping me get my new laptop set up. It was just the two of us in my office. In a quiet moment he shared his thoughts, "Mom, I don't' think I want to do engineering for a living. Everyone moans about money." I burst out laughing. I had to let him down easy. "Son, welcome to the world. This happens in all types of environments. You'll find that people moan about everything, especially money. You need to decide whether you are one of those moaners or you're one of those people who say I can change things and make a difference and you just get on with it."

Problem Solving is Essential In Today's Fast Paced World

The world is changing so quickly it's not possible for us to work out all of the answers. We don't even know all the questions. Vibrant organizations thrive on this demanding and evolving environment. They thrive on it and at the same time their survival depends on it. Today's problems are tomorrow's opportunities. Being able to think about potential new needs, requirements for new products or new information is an incredibly powerful tool.

Try to take a moment to think longer term about the trends in your own professional world, so you can capitalize on them and position your investments in your career accordingly. Also, take a moment to think about your family's potential longer-term needs. Are you in the neighborhood you want to be in? What's the best longer-term strategy for my kids' education? Are you happy with the mix of free time versus work time? Certain issues require more long-term planning, but it's these types of decisions which are likely to have the biggest impact on the quality of your life.

Career-Family Balance Demands Continuous Creativity

Problem solving is essential in all lifestyles. Finding solutions, however, is a *must have* when you adopt the career-family lifestyle. You've got two intense, complex lives to lead. Keeping those in balance is only possible through continuous creativity. This is why creating solutions is an undercurrent throughout this book.

When we looked at teamwork, one of the ways I mentioned that you support your partner is by helping them deal with problems at a work. You're the one standing on the outside looking in, and you can therefore offer a fresh perspective. In the chapter on getting the balance right, I admitted very frankly that this balancing act is not easy. You will have trials and tribulations thrown at you which you're just going to have to work through. Problems will arise, but you'll be determined to create solutions. When talking about the benefits of career and family, I asserted that kids not only benefit from a working mother's ability to sort things out, but that they also learn to solve problems for themselves. Spread the magic of problem solving in all aspects of your life. You'll find that it yields delightful surprises.

CHAPTER ELEVEN

The Bonus Chapter:
You Gotta Laugh

WHEN I COMPLETED THE OUTLINE for this book, a colleague wisely advised, "Christine, you can't end your book on problem solving. It's got to end with something sexier." She suggested that I come back to it after I started writing the book. It was frustrating that I couldn't nail the idea for the final chapter right at the beginning of the planning phase. I knew there was something missing, but I couldn't quite put my finger on it. Ah! It then came to me. Of course, how could I possibly forget? - It's *humor*! Best to keep this at the end anyway. If I had put it in the beginning of the book, you may not have taken me seriously.

Humor Brings Teams Together & Makes Work Fun

Humor is an essential ingredient in *all* aspects of life. That's right, *all* aspects. You may think that you need to have your serious face on when you go to work and then your humorous face on when you're with family and friends. On the contrary, humor is a very effective management tool for bringing teams together.

Humor makes work fun. It energizes people and makes them perform better. When people ask me how I worked on a trading floor for so long, I usually reply that it was the laughter and vibrant atmosphere that kept me going. When you're sitting next to someone else ten inches on either side of you for ten hours a day, you can't follow the norms of polite and reserved behavior. The only way to survive is to use humor.

Humor Eases Day-To-Day Communication

Humor at work eases the day-to-day communication. You don't need to let things get out of hand. Simply address issues as they arise, using humor to make your point. An English colleague of mine would remind me of my sometimes intense behavior by observing, "Christine, you've got that mean Philly Rocky Balboa face on." (I'm originally from the Philadelphia area, which is why he decided to use that epithet.) It was his way of saying, "Relax, we'll get the work done." He always made me laugh at myself. I never got mad or offended, which I might have done had he attempted to have a frank and somber conversation about my behavior.

Effective Managers Use Humor To Lead

Think about your own professional environment. Weren't you enjoying yourself more when the group was having a laugh? Didn't you feel like, hey, this job isn't so bad after all? We sometimes forget the power of humor. A number of studies have shown that leaders who use humor as part of their management style are rated more highly than those that don't. (Now that's a serious statement.) This makes sense intuitively as strong leaders often have strong personalities to match, often referred to as charisma. Effective leaders also use humor to deliver tough messages. They can get their message across very poignantly without the audience going away feeling offended. Humor can give the team a wake-up call without completely de-motivating them. It makes the sting less personal.

Humor Makes You More Likeable

Humor is also what makes us like one colleague more than another, sometimes without our realizing it. I noticed that when I had to select colleagues to do my peer reviews, I would generally gravitate towards the ones who had a good sense of humor. They were the ones who I tended to have stronger relationships with. They were the ones I preferred to interact with, particularly on a bad day.

I was recently asked to provide a reference to a headhunter for a colleague who worked in human resources. My feedback was glowing, not only because of my colleague's technical knowledge and skill set, but also because of her ability to motivate her team through humor. She developed a strong, tightly knit group. I could tell when I dealt with any individual on her team that the team stood united. Each team member spoke respectfully of the other, and they all admired their boss's ability to bring the best out of each of them. Her ability to see the funny side in most things allowed me to tackle thorny HR issues. It lessened the burden. HR issues are never fun, but she made them fun.

Humor Relieves Tension

Humor can serve as an effective icebreaker when you're in a tense situation. Perhaps you need to provide formal feedback to a team member face to face and you want them to relax. Formality can often make people tense, making them less receptive to your comments and observations. This is why many professional speakers will start their presentations with a joke. Their topic may be dry, boring even, but they want people to pay attention. Humor that's spontaneous rather than canned is most effective, but not all of us have that natural gift.

Humor Diffuses Conflict

Humor, applied in the right way, is effective at diffusing conflict. You need to be very careful, however, and think about the particular individual and how they might take it. In a conflict situation humor used in the wrong way can make matters worse. Sometimes there is a fine line between humor and an insult. You may need to choose your words and theme carefully so that your strategy doesn't backfire. Appropriate humor puts people in a good mood. When you're in a good mood, you're more open to resolving a dispute.

In choosing your humor, be sensitive about how receptive your target audience is likely to be about any humor related to gender, race, politics and/or religion. As an example, gender-related jokes in a male-dominated environment when there are women present, are generally de-motivating for women, which defeat the point of trying to use humor to *build* teams, rather than isolate individuals.

Humor Gets Your Message Heard

If you want to be in the spotlight, one of the easiest ways to attract attention is to say something funny. People are more likely to listen to what you have to say. We all suffer from information overload, even when we know that the information will benefit us.

Sesame Street applies this formula to perfection. Instead of sitting a kid down and trying to teach him or her how to count by rote, *Sesame Street* adds humor and context to enable kids to have a greater chance of remembering and understanding what they are being taught. Wouldn't you rather learn to count with Count Dracula than with some tedious paper exercises? And doesn't Big Bird motivate you to read more when you watch him hosting his *Reading Hotline? Sesame Street* humor is fantastically clever. It includes material for the older audience to enjoy as well. Parents can watch the show with their kids and be equally entertained.

Don't Take Yourself Too Seriously

We are all human. We are all imperfect. Showing your own vulnerability by making fun of yourself is a wonderful way to remind yourself and others that you are human. I hate not being perfect, but I know that's the way it is, so I've got to deal with it. One of my weaknesses (or strengths?) is how demanding I am on myself and on others. In a professional setting I'll often say to colleagues in a joking manner, "That's not done yet? We must have discussed that at least 5 minutes ago," knowing full well that the task at hand will take a number of days rather than minutes to complete. This approach worked really well in a team setting, where as the team leader I needed to show the team that I did expect great things from them, but at the same time expected them to push back when I wasn't being realistic about meeting deadlines.

As a result of showing your own vulnerability, friends, family and colleagues gain respect for you, rather than the other way around. That's the paradox. They respect you for sharing your weaknesses, rather than boasting about all the great things you've accomplished. Notice that people who are at pains to tell you about how great they are, actually cause the opposite effect. You go away wondering what underlying insecurity is causing them to put on all this bravado.

You Only Truly Have a Sense of Humor When You Can Take a Joke

My former boss and now good friend was a hard driving manager, but at the same time demonstrated a brilliant sense of humor. He would always preach to our London-based team about how business needed to take priority over planned vacations (which for him as an American was quite a common way of thinking). You have to understand, vacations in Britain are *sacred*, in stark contrast to the US. You don't really interfere with them, except in dire circumstances. When you give up a vacation in the US, you are considered to be a hero, committed and working for a greater cause. If you give up a vacation in the UK, you are considered a loser – nothing really going on in your life except work.

Our team knew that for several months running the boss had been busy planning a two-week vacation in Vietnam. "Ah," we thought, this would be a perfect time to play a joke on "Mazz" (That was his nickname. Most people on a trading floor have a nickname. Mine was simply "CBQ", except when I worked for a Japanese bank when it was transformed into "CBQ san"). We decided to get the Head of the Fixed Income division (our boss' boss) to help us play a joke on Mazz. The plan was for the head to call Mazz into his office and tell him he needed to cancel his vacation.

The head of the division, who also had a great sense of humor, gladly played along. When Mazz came out of the boss's office he looked shaken and pale. He came back to our desk and proceeded to tell us that the boss asked him to cancel his vacation. He continued in his best New York accent, "You see, you gotta do what you gotta do." We let him really feel the anguish of the situation. Minutes felt like hours. We were dying to tell him the truth. He looked completely shell shocked. Moments later the division head came out onto the floor and revealed all. It was a brilliant moment! Mazz had a good laugh at himself and we respected him for it. "It's the ability to take a joke, not make one, that proves you have a sense of humor," maintains the American author and journalist Max Eastman.

Humor At Home Brings You Back To Earth

Humor at home brings you back to earth. You may have some important position at work, but when you're home, you're just plain ol' Mom or Dad. Your kids will make fun of you and have fun with you, regardless of your fancy job title. Your partner, because they know you well, will also poke fun at you, and by doing so bring you back to earth. I'm actually very grateful for the way I'm made fun of at home. When my husband gets irritated with my high energy level, he reminds me with a big smile on his face, "Remember Christine, I don't work for you." That remark doesn't upset me or make me angry. Instead it resets my mood. I know I've got to slow down and let others do things at their own pace, not mine.

When using humor at home, tread carefully with teenagers. They can be extra sensitive about *everything*. Nonetheless, using humor can definitely reduce the tension. Instead of constantly getting into battles with our children about cleaning up their rooms, we sometimes use humor to get the point across. Over one of the school breaks our elder son had a few friends staying with him in his room. My husband popped his head in and remarked, "Son, what color is the carpet, green? I guess it's pretty well protected by all the clothes covering the floor?" Our son's friends thought my husband's remarks were hysterical. Our son, on the other hand, was embarrassed, but it did the trick. Once his friends left, he cleaned up his room and you could actually see the green carpet again.

Final Thoughts:
Where Do We Go From Here?

BY READING THIS BOOK I hope you see that you don't need to have an extraordinary talent to be happy and successful in a career *and* at the same time enjoy family life. Forget the idea that this is the exclusive domain of Superwoman. Career does not need to exclude family, although this was certainly the case in previous generations. When you follow both aspirations, it's amazing how your family can support your career and how your career can support your family.

As demonstrated throughout the book, the keys to success in both of these "lives" are the same. Strike the career-family balance that's right for you. Don't accept no for an answer. Follow your gut instinct and listen to your inner voice on what's best. Be assured that your decision to participate fully in a profession as well as in a family benefits you in many ways, as well as those around you. Continue to be true to yourself. The career-family combination will help you achieve this. It keeps you honest.

Build a strong team around you. Apply your sharpened principles of commitment, communication and conflict management to help you work through day-to-day issues. Support your busy lifestyle by being well organized. Your finely-tuned problem-solving skills will allow you to work your way out of many sticky situations. And finally, make sure you laugh and have fun. There will be plenty of opportunities for it.

In sum, there is no secret formula. Following these simple steps each day will result in a happy and fulfilled life. Best of luck and enjoy the journey!

References

CHAPTER 1

General

Brown-Quinn, Christine, *"Career & Family Survey"*, February 2010

Chittenden, Maurice, *"Jobs for the girls as the 'mancession' bites"*, The Sunday Times, 15 November 2009

Mills, Eleanor, *"The Second Sex"*, The Sunday Times Magazine, 15 November 2009

Shriver, Maria, *"The Shriver Report: A Study by Maria Shriver and the Center for American Progress"*, 2009

Education

Costello, Bill, *"Where the Education Gender Gap is Leading in America"*, Education Reporter, December 2008

Goudreu, Jenna and Tulshyan, Ruchika, *"Why More Women are Heading to Business School"*, and Forbes.com, 16 April 2010

Intini, John, "Female University Enrollment Exceeds Male", The Canadian Encyclopedia, 26 June 2006

Professional Fields

Arnst, Catherine, *"Are There Too Many Women Doctors?"*, Business Week, 17 April 2008

Gulli, Cathy & Lunau, Kate, *"Canada's Doctor Shortage Worsening"*, The Canadian Encyclopedia, 14 January 2008

Workplace

Bonthuys, Natalie, *"Making it Work: Balancing Career & Family"*, www.jobsinlondon.co.uk, 2009

Michaels, Nancy, *"Women Entrepreneurs Growing in Numbers & Importance"*, www.score.org, 2009

Monsebraaten, Laurie, *"In a shrinking workforce women outnumber men"*, www.thesstar.com, 5 September 2009

Newman, Judith, *"What Do Alpha Women Really Want?"*, www.marieclaire.com, April 2010

Northwest Regional Development Agency, *"UK's women entrepreneurs can lead us out of recession"*, Risk and Reward: the 6th Prowess Annual International Conference, 2009

Qureshi, Huma, *"New Female Breadwinners"*, The Guardian, 24 October 2009

Relax News, *The Independent, "Almost half of US women are primary breadwinners"*, 16 October 2009

The Economist, "Women in the Workforce: Female Power", 30 December 2009

The Sydney Morning Herald, "What do women really want? How to Capture Your Share of the Largest, Fastest Growing Market", 21 October 2009

Demographic Trends And Societal Attitudes

AFL-CIO, Department for Professional Employees, *"Fact Sheet 2006 - Professional Women: Vital Statistics"*

Batty, David, *"Divorce rate at its lowest for 26 years"*, www.guardian.co.uk, 29 August 2008

Blair-Loy, Mary, *"Competing Devotions: Career & Family Among Women Executives"*, Harvard University Press, 2005

Center for Disease Control, *www.cdc.gov/datastatistics*

Cheswich, Donna, *"Marriage and Divorce rates in the United States", www.examiner.com,* 25 October 2009

Drew, Amanda, *"Why Fewer Couples are Choosing to Tie the Knot", marriage.suite101.com,* 12 May 2009

Office for National Statistics, *www.ons.gov.uk*

Women Leaders

Cranfield Female FTSE 100 Report, November 2009

Ellison, Jess, *"Shattering the Glass Ceilings", www.newsweek.com,* 15 June 2010

CHAPTER 4

www.bbc.co.uk, "Diallalio names in RFU task force", 28 August 2009

Prynn, Jonathan, *"Renault boss quits in Formula One scandal over deliberate cash", London Evening Standard,* 16 September 2009

CHAPTER 9

Gapper, John, *"Lessons in Damage Control", Financial Times,* Business Spectator, 14 November 2009

CHAPTER 12

Heisser, Pattie, *"Barbara Sher: Career Counselor, Best Selling Author, Speaker, Pioneer", www.50fabulous.com,* 1 April 2009

Christine Brown-Quinn
THE FEMALE CAPITALIST™

INSPIRED by more than twenty years of balancing a high-powered career in international finance with an active family life, Christine founded The Female Capitalist™ in 2010. Through her consultancy practice Christine is committed to helping professional women achieve career-family success, as well as helping organizations reap the full benefits of female capital. Her book – *Step Aside Super Woman... Career & Family is for Any Woman* colorfully reveals how to strike the right balance between career goals and family aspirations, using a common set of values, strategies and skill sets.

Christine has an undergraduate degree in Foreign Languages from Georgetown University (Cum Laude) and an MBA in International Business from George Washington University (Beta Gamma Sigma scholar). She is also a tutor for Georgetown's Graduate Program in International Management at Oxford University. Her tutorials cover the issues of gender equality from a public policy perspective as well as managing diversity within the workplace.

**Christine
Brown-Quinn**

The Female Capitalist

Maximizing the Return on Female Capital

> *Is your organization reaping the full benefits of female talent?*

> *Could your professionals benefit from developing strategies for balancing career and family?*

Through corporate consulting, workshops, individual coaching and motivational speaking, The Female Capitalist™ can help you find win-win solutions for the individual *and* the organization.

Contact us to find out how ∨

Website address: www.christinebrown-quinn.com
Email address: christine@christinebrown-quinn.com

T: +44(0)1727 739899
M: +44(0)7785 550559

Author of **Step Aside Super Woman**
Career & Family is for Any Woman

Also available from Bookshaker.com

PRESENTING YOURSELF
─ WITH ─
IMPACT
AT WORK

How To Transform The Way You Communicate for Better Results

GILL GRAVES

"The Coaching Parent fills a significant gap in coaching literature. I was especially gratified to discover how much importance and space is given to the building of self-confidence in all its forms. This is the foundation stone for life and needs to be set early. Who better to do it than parents."

Sir John Whitmore, best selling author of "Coaching for Performance"

The Coaching Parent

Help Your Children Realise Their Potential by Becoming Their Personal Success Coach

David Miskimin and Jack Stewart

취업율 남 : 여 50% : 50%
Still 평균소득은 80% of men

20484083R00103

Made in the USA
Lexington, KY
06 February 2013